75 YEAR-ROUND HIKES IN NORTHERN CALIFORNIA

75 YEAR-ROUND HIKES

IN NORTHERN CALIFORNIA

Marc J. Soares

THE
MOUNTAINEERS
BOOKS

Published by
The Mountaineers Books
1001 SW Klickitat Way, Suite 201
Seattle, WA 98134

First edition, 2000.

Published simultaneously in Great Britain by Cordee, 3a DeMontfort Street, Leicester, England, LE1 7HD

Manufactured in the United States of America

Project Editor: Dottie Martin
Editor: Julie Van Pelt
Cover and Book Designer: Kristy L. Welch
Layout Artist: Kristy L. Welch
Mapmaker: Jennifer LaRock Shontz
Photographer: Marc J. Soares

Cover photograph: *Sawtooth Mountains from above Horseshoe Lake* © Marc Soares
Frontispiece: *Chaos Crags, Lassen Peak, and Manzanita Lake in late spring* © Marc Soares

Library of Congress Cataloging-in-Publication Data
Soares, Marc J.
    75 year-round hikes in Northern California : the ultimate guide for fall, winter, and spring hikes / Marc J. Soares.— 1st ed.
        p.   cm.
Includes index.
    ISBN 0-89886-720-7 (pbk.)
    1. Hiking—California, Northern—Guidebooks. 2. Trails—California, Northern—Guidebooks. 3. California, Northern—Guidebooks. I. Title: Seventy-five year-round hikes in Northern California. II. Title.
    GV199.42.C2 S634 2000
    917.94—dc21
                                                                    00-009643
                                                                    CIP

CONTENTS

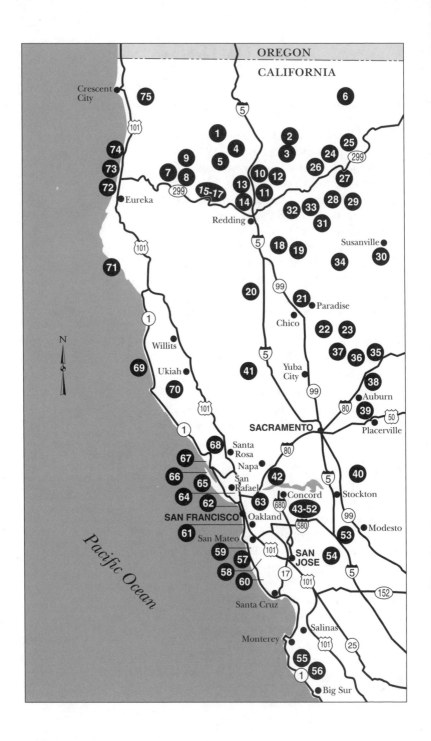

LEGEND

═══⑤═══	Interstate highway
───⟨101⟩───	U.S. highway
─⟨299⟩─⟨99⟩─	State highway or improved road
──────────	Road
- - - - - - - - - -	Dirt Road
- - - - - - - -	Trail
◄- - - - - - - -	Unhiked trail
··················	X-country trail

Symbol	Description	Symbol	Description
←	Directional symbol	⁚⁚	Springs
Ⓟ	Parking	⋕	Waterfall or cascade,
▮	Ranger station		including seasonal
■	Building	⚘⚘	Marsh or swamp
▲	Mountain	⌒	River or stream
●	Place of interest	=	Bridge
⅂⌐	Picnic area	❀	Spring wildflowers
▲	Car campground	⚘	Fall color
⌂	Backcountry campsite	❄	Winter snow

San Francisco Bay Area to Big Sur

Northern California Coast

INTRODUCTION

Off-season is a special time when nature is at its best. Autumn shows off the brilliant changes in leaf color. Winter is when the countryside gets green and the streams become powerful. Spring is peak wild-flower season. Off-season hiking means more seclusion, more tranquility, and more intimacy. As a kid living near Redding, where the summers are scorching hot, 95 percent of my hikes were off-season excursions. It was a treat to see flamboyant gold and crimson leaves, raging wild waters, and flower-carpeted hillsides.

In the off-season of Northern California, when temperatures are mostly mild, ranging from cool to pleasantly warm, hikers have more energy to enjoy the trails. The seventy-five carefully chosen hikes in this book are probably better when hiked in the off-season. You will avoid the long lines and crowded trails common to summer hiking, and you won't have to wait for the snow to melt from the higher country.

It's a privilege and an honor to hike in the off-season, and Northern California features arguably the greatest collection of ultimate off-season places to explore. *75 Year-Round Hikes in Northern California* offers a variety of hikes to achieve balance, and to provide plenty of choices. Choose from ridgetop hikes with breathtaking views, creek and lakeside strolls, beautiful excursions at the ocean's edge, tall red-wood encounters, and higher elevation mountain endeavors with chances to traipse in snow.

The intent of this book is for you to expand your hiking season, and in doing so, have more fun, be more comfortable, more informed, more motivated, and above all, more touched. This guidebook features hikes to suit all abilities and moods, with a blend of "cakewalks" and "buttkickers," backpacking trips, and family walks. Keep this book in the glove compartment during the drive for easy access. Then take it with you so you can read excerpts along the way.

HOW TO USE THIS BOOK

The hikes in this book are divided into seven geographical regions to help you in locating and choosing an excursion. The regions approximate a clockwise trip around the state, beginning near Mount Shasta and the Trinity Alps in the north, travelling south to Big Sur, and then moving north again along the coast to finish in glorious redwoods near Crescent City. You can also use the Trail Index at the back of the book

San Francisco skyline viewed from Angel Island, winter

to identify the best trip for you. Hikes are suggested for autumn, winter, and spring. There are also recommended trips to take with children, suggested backpacking adventures, and top bird-watching trails.

Each hike description is broken into four basic parts. A hike summary heads each chapter, and is followed by the trip's highlights, directions to the trailhead, and finally a guide to the route describing landmarks and trails. It's a good idea to read the entire hike description before choosing that hike and before actually hitting the trail. You'll find out about trail characteristics, where the tough climbs might be, how much shade might be offered, and important landmarks and special scenes you won't want to miss. The trail descriptions also often identify the most prominent native trees and shrubs, helping boost your native plant knowledge and awareness.

The hike summaries give you the following basic information about trip length and difficulty, elevation, maps, campgrounds, and who to call for more information.

Distance. This is the trip's mileage, specifying if the route is round trip, one-way, or a loop trip. Note that many of the longer hikes feature great scenes within a couple of miles, allowing people who lack time and/or energy to turn back early.

Difficulty. This category rates each hike as *easy, moderate,* or *strenuous.* These terms are somewhat subjective, factoring in distance, elevation gain, and trail conditions. Easy could seem moderate to a nonhiker while strenuous could seem moderate to a distance runner. Other factors can make hikes seem more difficult, such as heavy winds, soreness, or being thirsty or hungry. Some hikes rated strenuous might be easy for the first couple of miles, and therefore might make an ideal short hike. Many hikes are described as "easy to moderate" or "moderate to strenuous" in order to better approximate the difficulty factor.

High point and **elevation gain.** The high point is the highest elevation reached on a hike, while elevation gain is an approximate number of actual feet you'll climb from a trip's beginning to its end. This is often a better measure of difficulty than a hike's high point because total elevation gain factors in all of the ups and downs you'll encounter. Note that most hikers consider 1000 feet of gradual climbing much easier than 1000 feet of steep ascent.

Maps. US Geological Survey (USGS) 7.5' quadrangle topographic maps or US Forest Service (USFS) topographic maps are recommended for each hike and are given by name. These maps are available at most outdoor and sporting goods stores. In cases where the USGS or USFS maps are out of date or unavailable, alternate maps are suggested. A map is one of the Ten Essentials (see What to Bring) and, with a compass, can come in extremely handy if you become lost. Be aware that even recent topographic may not show newer trails. Maps accompany each hike description and show each route's trails, major place names, and main bodies of water. For getting to your destination, take along a California highway map or state atlas.

Nearest campground. This is the nearest car campground to the hike. Spending the night in an area gives you the option of perhaps doing more than one hike. The campgrounds given are open year-round unless otherwise stated. Most charge fees and at least have running water, but faucets and facilities may be restricted in winter months. Some campgrounds are actually primitive camps with no facilities. Call ahead. You may have a campground all to yourself during the off-season, especially on weekdays. Should you prefer even more solitude, keep in mind that there are frequently backpacking camps along the trails described.

Information. This is the governing agency that has jurisdiction over the area that includes the hike. A phone number is given so that you can call to determine permit

Teasel

requirements, user fees, and trail conditions. You may have to leave a message on a machine, so call well in advance of your trip.

YEAR-ROUND HIKING CONSIDERATIONS

Hiking year-round provides joys not found in summer, but there are also special considerations to keep in mind. Many parks and gates often close at dusk, so call ahead. Even if you do call, staff at parks and recreation areas might be off for the month or the season, and so there may be no assistance or information available.

Trail conditions and highlights vary with the season. Winter and early spring rains produce slick spots on trails. Spring brings on bolting grasses and new shrub growth, making for overgrown trails that provide happy havens for ticks (see Staying Safe). Hikes with far-reaching views should be done on clear days, which are most common in autumn. But trips through deep forest and heavy woods are often better enjoyed when done under the thick cloud cover or fog of winter and early spring.

Finally, days are shorter in the off-season, making long day hikes less feasible and sometimes causing you to rush. Several of the hikes in this book suggest a one-way option. This means arranging for a car to meet you at another trailhead. Car shuttles eliminate the return trip, allowing you to travel farther, see more, and take more time to enjoy the hike.

South Yuba River

WHAT TO BRING

The Ten Essentials are a must for every trip. They will keep you safer and will most likely heighten enjoyment. They include extra clothing (in layers, plus a thin poncho or light raincoat); extra food (especially complex carbohydrates); sunglasses; a knife; firestarter (for wet wood); matches in a waterproof container; a first-aid kit; a flashlight (with extra batteries); a map; and a compass. A whistle can also come in handy in emergency situations.

It's a good idea to leave most of these items in your daypack at all times, updating the first-aid kit and matches annually. For long and strenuous hikes, you'll need a pair of broken-in, lightweight hiking boots. An ankle-high tennis shoe with good-gripping soles is recommended. The sun can easily drain one's energy and cause sunburn, so in addition to sunglasses, wear a shirt, a wide-brimmed hat, and use sunblock. Other items that might make your trip more enjoyable are toilet paper, a watch, binoculars, and this book.

STAYING SAFE

Bears, rattlesnakes, and mountain lions are not even close to the biggest dangers you'll encounter on the trail, especially in the off-season. More hikers by far are harmed or even killed by bee stings. In off-season hiking, hypothermia, getting lost, or falling are the main dangers that hikers should take into account. Hiking can easily rate among the safest activities if you take the following advice and note the possible hazards listed.

Be prepared. Study maps beforehand. Keep your daypack full of the Ten Essentials (see What to Bring). Make sure you can handle the mileage and climbing of a given hike. Get the weather report.

Pay attention. AA stands for "always alert." Sprained ankles, perhaps the most common hiking injury, are most often caused when a hiker lets his or her guard down, usually on the way down. Assume that each step could result in a fall and be extra attentive to slippery rocks and mud. "Watch your eyes" means make sure branches don't poke you in the eye. Gather and break firewood carefully.

Make good decisions. If the watch indicates it'll be dark sooner than later, allow sufficient return time. If the creek is too swollen to cross, cross in a safer place or not at all. When you arrive at a trail junction, stop, study the map, and wait for the others. It's better to be a wuss than a stud.

Hiking alone. It's imperative to leave a hiking itinerary with someone and then stick to it. A solo hiker must maintain the mind-set that there is absolutely no room for error.

Water. A hiker will need up to one quart for every three miles traveled. Most developed campgrounds and recreation areas have drinking fountains or faucets, which provide the most reliable sources of potable water for hikers. However, many such amenities are restricted in the off-season. Assume that all water from streams, lakes, and ponds carries harmful microorganisms, including *Giardia lamblia,* which provokes stomach-flu-like symptoms. Always purify water from natural sources by using a filter that removes *Giardia*, by boiling briskly for 5 minutes, or by using iodine. If there's no developed water source near a hike, or streams and lakes are too murky or dry up, this is mentioned in the opening paragraphs of the hike description. It's always a good idea to bring plenty of your own water.

Weather. Always get an accurate and recent weather report. If a storm hits, you'll be ready with raingear and a waterproof tent. Keep your extra clothes dry by putting them in garbage bags inside your pack.

Poisonous plants. Poison oak and stinging nettles cause skin discomfort. Learn to recognize and avoid contact with these plants, even in winter. In the case of the more common poison oak, anyone can get it at anytime; even those who swear they never do. If poison oak is common along a trail, it will be mentioned in the hike description.

North Fork American River, early autumn

Lions and bears and snakes! Oh my! Use caution and things should be fine with black bears and rattlesnakes. In fact, most rattlesnake bites occur because people try to kill or handle them. If you encounter a mountain lion (rare), don't run, as sheep do. Stand your ground, look it in the eye, look big, and talk loud. Chances are that cat is already gone.

Ticks. Ticks are more of a problem than mountain lions, snakes, and bears combined. They live in brushy and grassy areas, with which hikers tend to come into contact. Check for ticks often if hiking along an overgrown trail (more common in mid-to-late spring). If a tick just comes aboard, it can be flicked off. If it's lodged, however, see a doctor. Some ticks carry Lyme disease, which makes people very sick.

ACKNOWLEDGEMENTS

Heavy praise and thanks to the following hiking folks, friends, and family who gave love, kindness, and inspiration to me:

Patricia Soares, Dionne Soares, Jake Soares, John Soares, Eric Soares, Camille Soares, Nancy Soares, Mozelle Berta, Les Berta, Rick Ramos, Derek Moss, Eric Pace, Nels Klaseen, William F. Nicol II, Anne Nicol, William F. Nicol IV, Ryan King, Alecia Kelly, and Bryan Buterbaugh.

MOUNT SHASTA AREA
AND THE TRINITY ALPS

1 ❧ HEART AND CASTLE LAKES

Distance: 3.4 miles round trip
Difficulty: Moderate
High point: 6000 feet
Elevation gain: 700 feet
Maps: USGS Seven Lakes, Dunsmuir; USFS Castle Crags Wilderness
Nearest campground: Castle Lake Campground, phone (530) 926-4511
Information: Mount Shasta Ranger District, Shasta-Trinity National
    Forest, phone (530) 926-4511

Mount Shasta is justifiably touted as special, even magical—a mountain full of good vibes that beckons harmonic convergence. This journey reveals numerous breathtaking views of the mountain, which will certainly convince hikers of these claims. This hike also shows the many facets of Castle Lake's sapphire waters, explores a verdant mountain meadow, and finally reaches precious Heart Lake, where the views of Mount Shasta and other prominent peaks are fantastic.

When there are drifts of lingering snow or after a first powder dusting, this alpine and subalpine region seems restful and serene, and may be negotiable with light boots. In deeper snow (most likely in January and February as well as in other cool months), the adventurous can don snowshoes and stay alert. In the event of any snow, call ahead

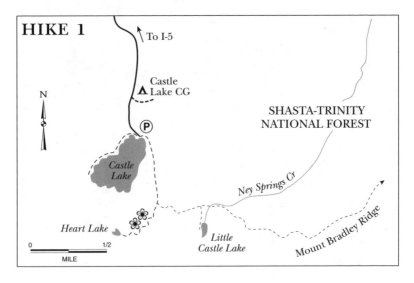

to at least make sure the road to the trailhead is open. Although this hike is often mostly clear of snow in April, conditions are still unpredictable. In 1998, snow covered Heart Lake into July. If you can reach the trailhead, you can always do the western shoreline hike of Castle Lake regardless of snowpack.

Be sure to learn more about this hike by reading the informative signboards at the northeastern edge of Castle Lake. They contain useful information about the lake's fish, geology, local and natural history. On an Indian summer day, you can still cleanse yourself of dust, sweat, and/or stress with a dip into crystal clear Heart or Castle Lake. Autumn is also a time of golden brown meadow grasses, faded flowers, and fewer folks.

Castle Lake and Black Butte

From I-5, take the Central Mount Shasta exit west then south to W.A. Barr Road and turn left. Cross Lake Siskiyou's dam 2.6 miles from the freeway exit, continue 0.2 mile, and turn left onto paved Castle Lake Road. Park in the large lot at road's end at 7.1 miles.

The trails to Heart Lake and Castle Lake begin near the Castle Lake outlet. Follow the trail to the right to walk the western shore of Castle Lake before climbing to Heart Lake. Castle Lake is a typical glacial cirque (semicircle lake), backed by an impressive castlelike stone wall. As with all cirques, Castle Lake is deepest near its steep rock wall, in this case up to 120 feet deep. Even in winter, a hiker can always negotiate the low evergreen shrubbery decorating the western shore of the lake. A good foot trail follows the lake's intimate and curving shoreline for 0.6 mile.

The shady parts of the trail provide ideal growing grounds for the lush and abundant western azaleas thriving beneath upright and slender lodgepole pines and red firs. The alternating sunny sections are a low carpet of greenleaf and pinemat manzanitas, chinquapin, and mountain spiraea. As you approach the granite cliffs, there's a small beach followed by a rocky perch—both spots are just right for experiencing the wind sweeping over Castle Lake's dark and shiny waters.

To get to Heart Lake, retrace your steps to the outlet, head south-east, cross a small stream, and then follow the rocky trail as it rises above Castle Lake. Look for white caps past western ninebark and huckleberry oak shrubs. Reach a rocky saddle 0.6 mile onto this trail, bear right (south) at a junction onto an unsigned trail over slabs of rock and proceed into a sloping and grassy meadow where yarrow, phlox, coyote mint, lupine, and paintbrush flourish in late spring.

At 0.5 mile past the trail junction, reach smallish Heart Lake with its interesting, boulder-laced shoreline interspersed with mountain spiraea and red mountain heather. A spur trail leads west past a couple of makeshift campsites to the safe side of a sheer and dark cliff face looking down onto Castle Lake. From Heart Lake's outlet, gorgeous views unfold of Mount Shasta, Black Butte, and Castle Lake (all in one scenic photo). Climb the ridge to the south by heading back into the meadow. Pick and choose your way first up the grassy slopes and then the talus to the manzanita- and chinquapin-choked ridge top. From here, you get the prime views just described, plus a stunning backdoor view of Castle Crags.

To extend the trip or for a great backpack trip, head back to the trail junction, follow the path east over the pass then down toward Little Castle Lake. While the lake itself is not even half as beautiful as Heart and Castle Lakes, the trail climbs beyond the Little Castle Lake turnoff through regal red firs to reach Mount Bradley Ridge, where the views are comparable to those from Heart Lake.

2 ⚘ McCLOUD RIVER'S THREE WATERFALLS

Distance: 3.2 miles round trip
Difficulty: Easy
High point: 3600 feet
Elevation gain: 200 feet
Map: USGS Lake McCloud
Nearest campground: Fowlers Camp Campground, phone (530) 964-2184
Information: McCloud Ranger District, Shasta-Trinity National Forest, phone (530) 964-2184

Tuning into a wild river boasting a trio of fantastic waterfalls on a hike that's a piece of cake seems too good to be true, but that's what you

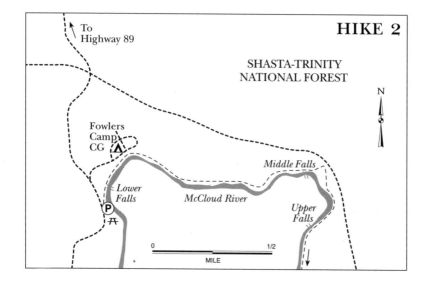

get with this journey. All three of these exhilarating falls are ringed in granite, but the similarities end there. Lower Falls are by far the tamest. Middle Falls exude a spiritual feel. A soul can easily hark back to the days when the Wintu Indians must have found deep peace on one of the big rocks at the scene. Upper Falls aren't as photogenic as Middle Falls, but are perhaps the most unique looking, and certainly carry the most water force. You'll most likely encounter people fishing along the way.

This hike definitely offers a lot for little energy expense. You can make it a much longer hike or even a backpack trip by continuing on a new trail section (built in the late 1990s) along the banks of the fast flowing McCloud River. After 14 miles you come out of a very remote river region into the tiny community of Algoma.

From I-5 south of Mount Shasta, take Highway 89 east 10 miles to McCloud. Drive 5 more miles and turn right onto the paved road signed for river access and Fowlers Camp Campground. Go 0.6 mile, continue straight at a road fork, bear right 50 yards farther, and continue 0.6 mile to the trailhead at the Lower Falls of the McCloud River picnic area.

Up to 40 feet wide in late spring, Lower Falls of the McCloud River (the hike's starting point) spill 15 vertical feet, forming a foamy avalanche of white froth that pours into a 25-yard-long pool. Picnickers and fishermen relax along the granite slab field overlooking the inspirational scene. Daredevil youngsters sometimes leap from the rocky edge 15 feet into the swirl.

A wide asphalt path follows the raging river upstream, past serviceberry, snowberry, thimbleberry, and ferns roofed mainly by Douglas fir and occasional incense cedar, white fir, and ponderosa pine. Manzanita and ceanothus shrubs highlight the sunnier sections. The frequent views down on the river are serene in the autumn and early winter, and provocatively wild in the spring.

Fowlers Camp Campground borders this narrow channel of clear and cold water starting at 0.2 mile. Long ago, the Wintu Indians camped here seasonally to fish and hunt. Black oak, hazelnut, and dogwood join the forest as the trail converts to a wide dirt path at 0.4 mile.

Soon after you note an eroded and steep cliff face on the other shore at 0.8 mile, look for the 20-foot tall, rare Pacific yew conifer (peeling, madronelike trunks and redwoodlike needles) at trailside. Shortly, you'll see, but not hear, a fast moving sheet of white just beyond a big rock outcrop so imposing, it causes the course of the river to veer.

Set in a steep and rocky canyon dotted with majestic Douglas firs, rectangular-shaped Middle Falls of the McCloud River are some 30 yards wide with a spectacular drop-off half that distance. When a north breeze kicks up, the mist is heavenly in your face. Even from a distance, a soul can get outright but refreshingly wet by sitting on one of several large boulders across from the falls. On many sunny midafternoons, a small rainbow forms on the left side of the falls.

Middle McCloud Falls, midspring

From Middle Falls, the trail snakes up and away, reaches a prime vista down on the falls, ascends some long, wooden steps, and culminates on a rocky rim covered with manzanita and interspersed with squaw carpet. Check out a clear view of the falls from a nearby rocky perch beneath a cluster of ponderosa pines. The surging white water in the canyon resembles a wild scene from the Colorado River. Look forward to pleasing views of Mount Shasta and mountains along the Trinity Divide along this stretch of the return route.

Inspirational and longing looks down into the river continue for another 0.25 mile or so. At 1.4 miles you reach a shady section featuring a staggeringly steep wall of lichen-coated gray rock on the left side of the trail. The first sighting of the Upper Falls of the McCloud River promptly ensues just past this 20-foot-high corridor.

Hemmed in on both sides by steep granite cliffs, these falls are an extremely powerful chute of pure white water. Looking down on the surging water, it's easy to imagine a bursting dam. Make your way down the spur trail to the edge of a large, round swirling pool (ideal for trout fishing). Retrace your steps and wander over to the falls' lip, where you'll be mesmerized by the 100-yard-long all-white cascade hurrying to plunge over the edge.

3 SQUAW VALLEY CREEK

Distance: 6.6 miles round trip; 5.6 miles round trip to final falls
Difficulty: Easy to moderate
High point: 2500 feet
Elevation gain: 500 feet
Maps: USGS Girard Ridge, Yellowjacket Mountain
Nearest campground: Fowlers Camp Campground, phone (530) 964-2184
Information: McCloud Ranger District, Shasta-Trinity National Forest, phone (530) 964-2184

Remote and shaded, this flat trail takes you into a unique wilderness, noisy yet peaceful. Squaw Valley Creek is a constant barrage of boisterous waterfalls, crashing cascades, and roaring rapids. Many people enjoy fishing along the creek. The shorelines are hemmed by dark and spectacular basalt rock bluffs that interrupt the water's flow, and the usually moist slopes are coated with a thick blanket of mosses.

The birds-eye views of this creek are as constant as its vigorous

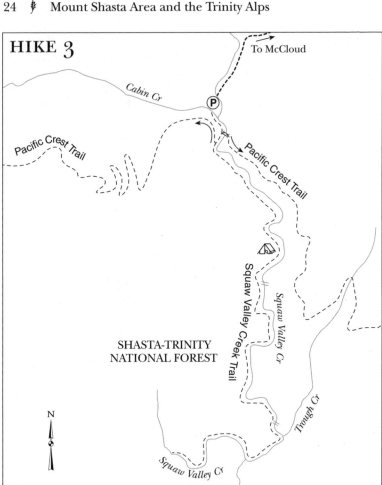

rapids, which in winter and spring sound like TV static. By September, the flow has receded enough that occasional small swimming pools are formed, inviting a dip.

The trip stays mainly in a mixed conifer forest, featuring plentiful mature Douglas fir and occasional incense cedar and bigleaf maple. Sun filters through the taller trees to dogwood (flowers here in early May), vine maple, black oak, shrubby canyon live oak, and Pacific yew (peeling, madronelike trunks and redwoodlike needles). The dogwoods, maples, and oaks create a flashy color display in the fall. Rotting logs, boulders, and shrubs dot the canyonside landscape, including currant, wild rose, red huckleberry (along the first 0.2 mile), a patch of Oregon grape (at 1.5 miles), ocean spray, and snowberry. Hartweg's ginger, ferns, iris, skyrockets, and bleeding hearts mingle with the mosses and banana slugs on the dark forest floor. Indian rhubarb, with leaves the size of elephant's ears, form umbrellas while growing in and along the creek.

From I-5, drive Highway 89 east exactly 10 miles into McCloud. Turn right on Squaw Valley Road, drive 5.9 miles, and turn right onto dirt Squaw Valley Creek Road. After 3.1 miles, park in the lot just past the bridge.

The unsigned trail crosses a bridge and quickly reaches another bridge that leads left to the Pacific Crest Trail. Continue straight, and reach a campsite at 1.3 miles. A bit farther, a trio of miniature water-falls blasts over a wide creek expanse. At full force in the spring, the nearest minifalls gush into a frothy whirlpool; the middle falls cata-pult into a small circular pool; and the final falls cascade into a swift current. Another 75 yards downstream, a huge, jagged basalt rock outcrop provides a perfect perch for admiring a 50-yard-long series of cascades. A spur trail snakes down to a 15-foot tall and equally wide waterfall at 1.8 miles, featuring a lushly moss-coated grotto/perch.

Just before reaching the point where Trough Creek plunges pre-cipitously into Squaw Valley Creek, the main trail reaches a final water-fall at 2.8 miles, which explodes powerfully off the rocks next to a tall alder tree. The last 0.5 mile breaks into a black oak woodland deco-rated by whiteleaf manzanita, redbud, and styrax shrubs, leading fi-nally to a rocky gulch where the trail ends abruptly.

Squaw Valley Creek, spring

4 ✤ CASTLE CRAGS AND INDIAN SPRINGS

Distance: 6.4 miles round trip; 3.6 miles round trip to Indian Springs
Difficulty: Strenuous, especially the final 0.7 mile
High point: 4800 feet
Elevation gain: 2300 feet
Maps: USGS Dunsmuir; USFS Castle Crags Wilderness
Nearest campground: Castle Crags State Park Campground, phone
   (530) 235-2684
Information: Castle Crags State Park, phone (530) 235-2684

From out of nowhere, the Castle Crags rise suddenly out of the peaceful forest, causing some to momentarily wonder if they've entered the twilight zone. Even more hikers marvel at how delightfully out of place these countless crags and spires seem to be. To show how tricky mountains can appear, vistas along this hike render the missile-shaped Castle Dome almost as big as Mount Shasta in the distance. Height and girth statistics reveal the truth, of course, but the illusion makes the dome and the taller crags in this low elevation, alpinelike zone even more breathtakingly ominous.

The incessant climb (some folks use the term relentless) begins in a peaceful and shady forest, with a visit to the cool and clear waters of isolated Indian Springs serving as a deserved break at halfway point.

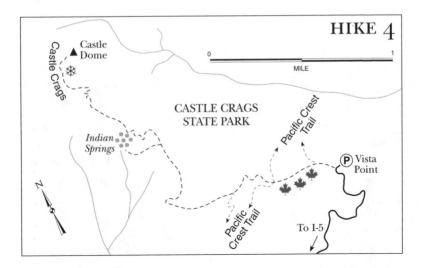

HIKE 4

Castle Crags, midspring

Two-thirds of the total hike are filled with view after view of the nearby Klamath Mountains (including the crags) and Cascade Range (including Mount Shasta). You'll be reaching for the camera frequently.

From I-5 some 6 miles south of Dunsmuir and 48 miles north of Redding, take the Castle Crags State Park exit. Go west 0.25 mile and turn into the park at the signed entrance. Follow all signs on the winding, paved road more than 1 mile up to the vista point. Then walk back down the road 50 yards to the trailhead. On the first part of the journey, walk in a mixed forest of Douglas fir, giant incense cedar, sporadic dogwood, and occasional black oak, Sadler oak, and canyon live oak. In early spring look for shooting stars (purplish flowers) and Indian warrior (reddish flowers) poking through the needle- and twig-littered forest floor.

At 1.3 mile, the trail flattens, ushering in a surprise view of Castle Crags. The continuous views westward to Gray Rocks aren't too shabby either. Snow lingers on the Gray Rock range usually into May.

This view becomes more commanding when you take the 0.25-mile long spur trail (left) at 1.6 miles to Indian Springs. The trail carves through an impressive thicket of whiteleaf manzanita dotted with ponderosa pines to the base of some gray rock obtrusions (the southern edge of Castle Crags). Quietly seeping miniature waterfalls decorate a huge moss-covered rock slab, comprising Indian Springs. In a neighboring gulch, water trickles past the partial dam made by a gargantuan Douglas fir that went down in the winter of 1997–98. Bigleaf maples tower over mature dogwoods and juvenile cedars here.

Back on the main trail, inaugural views of Mount Shasta appear as the shade vanishes. A maze of switchbacks escorts you into Castle Crags proper, resembling the stark gray walls and steep cliff faces that typify the Sierra Nevada. The crags continue to jut impressively over the final 0.5 mile. Bush chinquapin ekes out a hearty existence through cracks, crevices, and pockets. Ponderosa pine and Douglas fir outnumber the sugar pine and white fir.

From near the base of Castle Dome, numerous minidomes, mini-castles and minarets serve as ideal perches for gazing at Mount Shasta, Bradley Ridge in front of it, and Girard Ridge to the east. Most of these lookouts are much safer to scramble atop than the dome itself. There are several flat picnic spots amidst stunted Jeffrey pines. Enjoy an abundance of leaf colors changing in autumn, and be ready to delight in the snow, which can grace the high reaches of this hike in winter.

5 ⚜ BURSTARSE FALLS AND UGLY CREEK

Distance: 6 miles round trip
Difficulty: Easy to moderate
High point: 3250 feet
Elevation gain: 900 feet
Maps: USGS Dunsmuir; USFS Castle Crags Wilderness
Nearest campground: Castle Crags State Park Campground, phone (530) 235-2684
Information: Mount Shasta Ranger District, Shasta-Trinity National Forest, phone (530) 926-4511

Few folks know about this precious and mighty waterfall that free-falls some 50 feet over dark granite walls. This journey covers an impressive

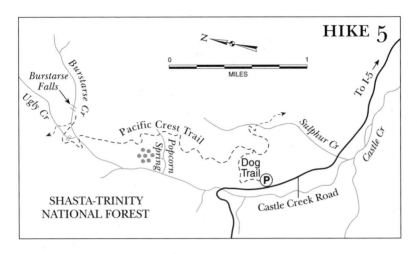

Z

0   1
MILES

Burstarse
Falls

Burstarse Cr

Ugly Cr

Pacific Crest Trail

Spring

Popcorn

Dog
Trail (P)

Sulphur Cr

Castle Cr

To I-5

SHASTA-TRINITY
NATIONAL FOREST

Castle Creek Road

2.5-mile stretch of the Pacific Crest Trail, laden with views of surrounding rocky-topped mountains, including the photogenic southwest faces of Castle Crags. Come in late winter through midspring and be fascinated with Ugly Creek's numerous cascades along two crossings. Standing beneath the spray of the falls is an unforgettable experience, but getting there involves some steep scrambling and being near a bit of poison oak. This trail is also open to horses.

From I-5 some 6 miles south of Dunsmuir and 48 miles north of Redding, take the Castle Crags State Park exit. Drive west on paved Castle Creek Road for 3.3 miles. Park in the large dirt lot on the right.

Unsigned Dog Trail takes off from the northwest side of the parking lot, climbing first past knobcone pines and then breaking through a chaparral of ceanothus, coffeeberry, and whiteleaf manzanita interspersed with canyon live oak, incense cedar, ponderosa pine, and Douglas fir. The bulk of the climbing is over once you reach the signed Pacific Crest Trail at 0.6 mile, where heading to the right for a level 0.25 mile yields a splendid view of Castle Crags.

The way to the falls goes left at the Pacific Crest Trail junction, showing off southerly views of Flume Creek Ridge and Gray Rocks, which are spectacular when snowcapped (usually from December through April). At 1.6 miles, reach a modest miniwaterfall at shady Popcorn Spring, followed by an unnamed stream where crystal water slides down a canyon over moss-covered rocks. Mostly shaded, level, and rocky, the Pacific Crest Trail is typically littered here with canyon live oak and occasional black oak acorns, Douglas fir cones, and canyon live oak leaves, which shed most of the year. Huckleberry oak

shrubs and greenleaf manzanita occupy much of the understory.

Reach the union of Burstarse and Ugly Creeks at 2.2 miles, where white water careens, glides, and spills gracefully over solid rock in late winter and early spring. Cross here and look for a cluster of western azalea nestled along the other shore. As the trail switchbacks and briefly climbs, look to the southeast for a rare view of Castle Crags and slender Burstarse Falls just across the canyon. Note from several vantage points along the trail how the long falls against a pure rock backdrop resemble a waterfall setting in Yosemite National Park.

Slim and gorgeous Ugly Creek features a long stretch of mostly white water in midwinter and spring, bounding over slick gray rock where it crosses the trail at 2.6 miles. Upon reaching the 180-degree turn on the trail, consider continuing some 100 yards to reach a splendid cascade in an open area of Ugly Creek (good views and a nice picnic spot). Otherwise, head toward the falls from the small clearing at the previously mentioned hairpin turn. Stay level for the first 40 yards as you pick and choose your way on a scant trail, descend gradually to the creek's edge then head for the bottom of the falls.

6 ✦ CALLAHAN LAVA FLOW AND WHITNEY BUTTE

Distance: 7.2 miles round trip
Difficulty: Moderate
High point: 5000 feet
Elevation gain: 600 feet
Map: USGS Lava Beds National Monument
Nearest campground: Indian Well Campground, phone (530) 667-2282
Information: Lava Beds National Monument, phone (530) 667-2282

The Modoc Indians were massacred here in a terrible war in 1872, but their spirits seem to linger over Lava Beds National Monument. This is a sacred land that at least metaphysically still belongs to these Indians. You're invited to reflect on these notions while hiking the same territory roamed by the Modoc Indians, just a few lava stone throws away from an actual battle site.

Your hike has a miles-from-nowhere feel, starting at the Merrill Ice Cave, one of several caves you can easily explore while at Lava Beds National Monument. Early winter is an ideal time to look for

Burstarse Falls, midspring

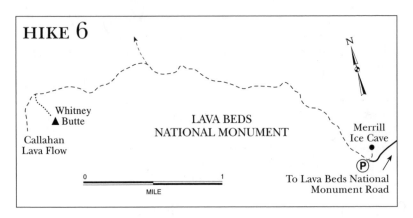

large mule deer near the trail. When there is snow here, the landscape can sometimes look like a cross between a sci-fi movie and a photo negative. Bring a camera to capture this mostly flat but bumpy land in front of Mount Shasta from a rare eastern vantage point. There is no water along the trail, so bring your own.

Drive Highway 299 east to Canby (133 miles from Redding). Turn north on Highway 139, drive 20 miles, and turn west on paved Lava Beds National Monument Road. Reach the visitor center after a few miles, continue 2.1 miles, and turn west again at the sign for Merrill Ice Cave. Park in the lot when this paved road dead-ends 0.9 mile farther. The slender dirt trail first heads mostly north through a flat and grayish desert motif of low-growing shrubs. California sage dominates, but there is also bitterbrush, rabbitbrush, and occasional mountain mahogany. Knee-high native bunchgrasses turn to golden hues in autumn, their clusters halted by lava rock piles that adorn the open and shadeless landscape. Western junipers come in all sizes here, from waist high to ten-yard tall stand-alone specimens.

An array of odd-shaped and geologically intriguing cinder cones, buttes, and domed peaks accentuate the countryside in all directions. With this mix of low shrubs and lava rock clusters, one moment you can feel like you're hauntingly in the middle of the Nevada desert, while the next moment is like moon exploration.

Several room-sized lava rock boulders coated with crustose lichens appear on the right at 1.7 miles. Choose one to scramble up and acquire a spectacular panorama. Note the striking contrast of two angular mountains—Shasta (west) and McLaughlin (north)—with the area's scattered domes, cones, and buttes.

Elongated dome-shaped Whitney Butte is enticingly close here, beckoning to be conquered. A westward view of Mount Shasta is precious and unique, accentuated by the linear rim stretching below Whitney Butte's southern flank. This scene at sunset is pure heaven.

When you regain the trail, pause to marvel at an 18-foot-tall juniper with 4 feet of its bottommost trunk totally encased in large lava rocks. Reach a trail fork at 2.2 miles and go left. Then round Whitney Butte 1 mile farther. The trail soon ends at Lava Beds National Monument's largest and most impressive sheet of basalt—Callahan Lava Flow. Covering many square miles, this bumpy field of dark gray boulders was extruded from Cinder Butte to the south over 1,000 years ago.

To climb Whitney Butte (a cinder cone), double back 100 yards or so, and then pick and choose your way a couple hundred feet to the summit, scattered with conifers and with superb views in all directions. Look east and north and admire Gillem Bluff and Schonchin Butte (they both can be easily reached after short hikes of about 1 mile).

Back at your car, grab a flashlight and follow the numerous steps down into Merrill Ice Cave to eventually reach an ice lake. Cold air sinks into the cave in winter and freezes the water, and the lake remains frozen for most of the year. There's a labyrinth of caves at the visitor center and several others within the park, all marked on the free map available from the visitor center.

High desert in Lava Beds National Monument

7 🌿 CANYON CREEK WATERFALLS

Distance: 16 miles round trip to Canyon Creek Lakes; 11 miles
round trip to Upper Falls; 7.2 miles round trip to Lower Falls
Difficulty: Moderate to strenuous
High point: 5700 feet
Elevation gain: 1800 feet to Lower Falls; 3400 feet to the lakes
Maps: USGS Mount Hilton, Dedrick; USFS Trinity Alps Wilderness
Nearest campground: Eagle Creek Campground, phone (530) 246-1225
Information: Weaverville Ranger District, Shasta-Trinity National
Forest, phone (530) 623-2121

Canyon Creek Trail has more highlights than coming attractions at
the movies. Stupendous views of a gin-clear Canyon Creek are topped
by visits to three totally different waterfalls, with a large and lush green
meadow accenting the halfway point. Go far enough and you'll be
surrounded by the steep, jagged gray granite peaks aptly named
Sawtooths. Canyon Creek Lakes are precious emerald gray jewels en-
trenched in the bottom of a stark high mountain canyon, and they
reflect ominous Sawtooth Mountain rising from the east. Although
both lakes are below 5700 feet (among the lowest of all forty-three
lakes in the Trinity Alps), they are affected by a colder than usual
microclimate, and thus subject to subalpine conditions, especially in

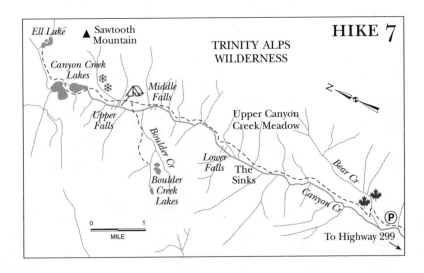

winter. The rare weeping spruce and foxtail pine, normally found at higher elevations, exist in this rugged area. In winter, the lakes are usually powder white with snow, although their granite banks remain bare, and snowshoeing the last mile or so up to the lower lake is doable if necessary.

This hike is ideal for the off-season, mainly because the throngs of folks in the summer have vanished. In autumn, when the canyonsides are adorned with glorious fall color, the creek is slow and lazy, showing off large boulders. In spring, as the snow melts from high side canyons, swollen side streams turn Canyon Creek into a loud and reckless surge of churning water, making spring the best time to admire the trio of blasting falls. Note that Canyon Creek is a popular fishing spot, and hikers share the trail with horses.

From Weaverville, continue west on Highway 299 8 miles to Junction City. Turn north onto Canyon Creek Road and drive 15 mostly paved, winding miles to the road's end.

Soon after starting on the trail, dogwoods and bigleaf maples near the boulder-hop crossing of Bear Creek (0.3 mile) offer a glorious mix of yellow and brilliant red in autumn. After a steep haul out of the canyon, wander into an open mountainside forest of madrone, Douglas fir, ponderosa pine, black oak, and occasional incense cedar. A bench in more lush forest at 1.4 miles features decent campsites, but is far from Canyon Creek, which you can view in its splendor far below in the canyon just 0.5 mile farther along the trail. A side trail on the left leads down to McKay Camp at 2.8 miles, followed by a view of a huge rockslide into Canyon Creek, which created a series of swirling pools called The Sinks (note the wild scar on the west bank).

Climb past a lichen-carpeted granite wall, cross a meandering stream three times (the last crossing is the obvious choice for getting water), and watch for a campsite on the left at 3.8 miles. From here, view a small waterfall cascading into a round pool, but be sure to mosey downstream to picnic at Lower Falls. Up to twice as wide as they are tall, these falls crash over a boulder pile into a deep pool before turning into rapids.

Canyon Creek Trail now climbs gently past a tall fern community before entering corn-lily-covered Upper Canyon Creek Meadow at 4.8 miles. Cross several tributaries, and climb through forest past some good creekside campsites to a spur trail branching left at 5.5 miles. This side trail promptly leads to Middle Falls near where Boulder Creek merges with one of many Canyon Creek channels below. A spectacular, discordant symphony of spray and rushing white water, the Middle

Falls plunge over a steep, terraced granite wall. In autumn, the onslaught of water is reduced enough that you can sit on one of the "steps" of this massive gray wall.

Walk about 0.5 mile and pass Boulder Creek and a trail leading left to Boulder Creek Lakes. Then in another 0.5 mile, your ears will guide you to misty Upper Falls, where a nice camp spot sits beneath red firs. It's a moderate 1-mile climb past brush and boulders to the lower of the Canyon Creek Lakes. You can go a bit farther to Ell Lake to extend the hike.

One of Canyon Creek's small, midspring waterfalls

8 ✣ SWIFT CREEK TO MUMFORD MEADOW

Distance: 14 miles round trip; 9 miles round trip to Parker Meadow
Difficulty: Moderate
High point: 5400 feet
Elevation gain: 2000 feet
Maps: USGS Covington Mill, Ycatapom, Siligo Peak
Nearest campground: Eagle Creek Campground, phone (530) 623-2121
Information: Weaverville Ranger District, Shasta-Trinity National
   Forest, phone (530) 623-2121

This trip is about admiring the loudest, fastest-flowing creek and the longest, greenest stretch of meadows in the entire Trinity Alps. Fittingly named Swift Creek, this hike's constant companion changes from a sometimes scary flow encased by a steep gorge of solid rock to a continual series of crystal currents alternating with inviting swim holes.

If it's late winter or spring, look and listen for waterfalls and cascades crashing against and over huge boulders along the first 3 miles of this hike. Wear boots during this time, and expect to negotiate mucky areas, especially where Swift Creek settles down in the meadows farther on.

Even in early autumn, the meadows can still be surprisingly green, and the swimming holes are refreshingly cold but comfortable enough to stay in for a short while. In summer, these meadows are often the

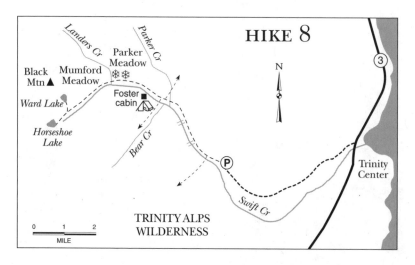

most populated place in the Trinity Alps, with families camping, avid fishermen working hard for trout, and groups of riders heading up the trail on horses. In the off-season, when new snows often cover the surrounding metamorphic rock mountains with shiny powder, you could have this paradise to yourself except for a few snowshoers.

From Trinity Center on Highway 3, turn west at the Swift Creek Trail sign. Travel 6.8 miles, following all signs for Swift Creek trailhead (always stay on the main road at forks) on a good, mostly dirt road.

The first highlight on the trail is a mix of pools and cascades rumbling over granite slabs at 0.7 mile. This is just past some good campsites on a bench above Swift Creek. Soon heavy-duty climbing ensues around a steep and narrow gorge that Swift Creek has cut through solid metamorphic rock. Walk to overhanging outcrops to look down on a pair of waterfalls at 1.5 miles. A bit farther, a sign on an incense cedar indicates the trail to Granite Lake, but stay right on the Swift Creek Trail, soon climbing gently past Douglas fir, ponderosa pine, incense cedar, and western azalea (white flowers in spring).

Cross several creeks, some of them willow lined, that eventually empty into Swift Creek, reach a small meadow, traipse through a heavily forested flat, and finally come to Parker Creek's impressive gorge at 4.2 miles. The towering Trinity Alps debut here and remain in view for the rest of the way. Go right a couple hundred yards farther at the

sign indicating Foster Cabin. Go left at another trail fork just beyond, and enter Parker Meadow at 4.7 miles.

Campsites abound from here on out, most in the meadows, under scattered firs and pines and near Swift Creek. Look for a surprising abundance of the rare California pitcher plant poking through extra moist patches of Parker Meadow. Foster Cabin hides deep in the open forest 0.4 mile into Parker Meadow. If rough weather hits, it's comforting to know there are bunks, a potbellied stove, and shelter from the storm here.

A tributary of Swift Creek, early autumn

The scattered incense cedars and ponderosa pines become more gigantic after crossing Landers Creek at 5.9 miles, where a 2-mile stroll ensues through lovely Mumford Meadow. Swift Creek dwindles the farther you go. At the west end of corn-lily-covered Mumford Meadow, it stays near the trail. A spur trail leads right to Ward Lake. The main trail climbs to Horseshoe Lake at 7 miles (a beauty if time and weather permit), the source of Swift Creek.

9 BIG BEAR LAKE

Distance: 8.4 miles round trip
Difficulty: Moderate to strenuous
High point: 5800 feet
Elevation gain: 2800 feet
Maps: USGS Tangle Blue; USFS Trinity Alps Wilderness
Nearest campground: Eagle Creek Campground, phone (530) 623-2121
Information: Weaverville Ranger District, Shasta-Trinity National Forest, phone (530) 623-2121

To capture the essence of the Trinity Alps in half the time and effort of the previous route, take this scenic hike. A northeast neighbor of the Trinity Alps core, Big Bear Lake is arguably the prettiest of its outer lakes. A possible tradeoff is that there is only one good campsite at the lake—if it's occupied, you'll have to come up with a plan B for camping.

Bear Creek is at its prettiest over the first mile, and the trail shows off several small falls, cascades, rapids, and clear swimming pools where fishermen may linger. Landscape variety is another strong point of this hike. You pass through dry oak woods, in and out of forests, across minimeadows and seeps, and finally over glacier-polished rock slabs. The views farther up are photogenic. Snow usually graces the final 1000 feet of the moderate climb during winter, which makes snowshoers happy. In midautumn, the black oaks and the occasional dogwoods offer trailside color.

From Highway 3, take Bear Creek Loop Road (dirt and old asphalt) 1.2 miles to the signed trailhead 100 yards south of a bridge. This access road is 15 miles north of Trinity Center. Cascades from Bear Creek unite with a slender waterfall from a feeder stream just before reaching a recently built bridge at 0.9 mile. Unbelievably tall twin white alders tower over the wooden walkway and unveil scenes of water rushing over large boulders. Typical of the Trinity Alps main

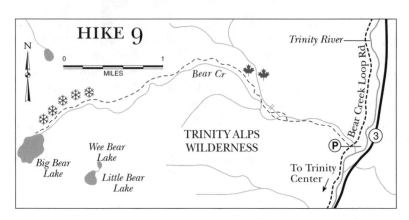

creeks, Bear Creek is a torrent of swiftly moving, bubbly white water that wears down a profuse, scattered battlefield of granite boulders.

The trail continues its moderate climb, now snaking away from the creek and along a woodland slope dominated by youthful black oaks. Pure stands of greenleaf manzanita are interrupted by ceanothus and huckleberry shrubs and the occasional knobcone pine. Sugar pine, incense cedar, and Douglas fir predominate more and more as you reunite with the creek at 1.7 miles.

For the next mile, the trail stays within easy earshot but just out of view of Bear Creek, alternating between stately forests and modest swales green with ferns and grasses. The trail then cuts through chaparral at 2.8 miles and climbs away from the creek. Sightings now unfold of the steep granite rock walls that encase the Bear Lakes and typify the naturally rugged Trinity Alps ridge tops. Small but scintillating waterfalls pour gracefully down the smooth slabs in late winter and spring.

After climbing out of a forest, you reach an alder thicket at 3.3 miles, and splendid views of spirelike minarets to the northwest. Trail negotiation the rest of the way is slowed by attractive little seeps and springs, pretty but at times overgrown with western azalea and ocean spray, or covered by the sporadic downed conifer. Be alert, double back to find the trail if necessary, and check for ticks. If snow becomes an impediment, you may have to play it safe and turn back, but the views to the east of Mounts Shasta and Eddy make the shortened journey worthwhile.

Once you reach wide-open granite rock, chances are you'll be drawn to this very wide section of Bear Creek as it meanders gently over the polished granite. Twenty-eight-acre Big Bear Lake resembles a cross between Papoose and Canyon Creek Boulder Lakes, both in the heart of the Trinity Alps. Tucked into a glacial cirque and granite-hemmed from all sides except east, Big Bear Lake has few trees adorning the shoreline. They include western white pine, mountain hemlock, and red fir. It's a real treat at sunrise or sunset to scramble quickly up to some boulders near the lake's driftwood-clogged mouth to adore prime views of Mounts Shasta and Eddy to the east. By picking and choosing your way east around a peak, then veering southwest, it takes about 1 mile cross-country to reach Little Bear and Wee Bear Lakes.

Mount Eddy as seen from Big Bear Lake, midspring

REDDING, SHASTA LAKE, AND WHISKEYTOWN LAKE

10 🌿 BAILEY COVE LOOP TRAIL

Distance: 3.5 miles round trip
Difficulty: Easy
High point: 1150 feet
Elevation gain: 400 feet
Map: USGS O'Brien
Nearest campground: Bailey Cove Campground, phone (530) 275-1589
Information: Shasta Lake Ranger District, Shasta-Trinity National
   Forest, phone (530) 275-1589

This family hike explores the shoreline of a prominent peninsula which was once a mountain. The well-constructed trail is short enough to attract fishermen, who cast out lines along the numerous minicoves that grace this scenic journey. Mountain bikers also use this trail. The sprawling docks of Holiday Harbor appear past Douglas firs on the outer stretches of narrow Bailey Cove. This large collection of houseboats

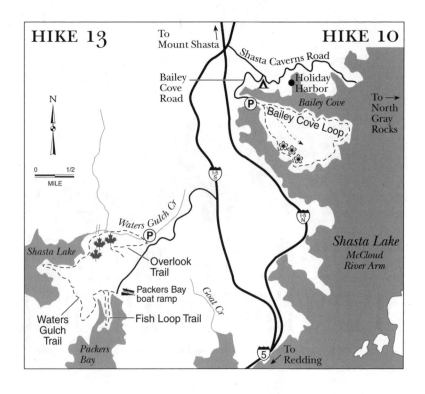

Limestone formations from Bailey Cove, winter

is as tranquil as a ghost town in the rainy season. The views near the mouth of Bailey Cove make splendid photos. The phenomenal limestone formations across the clear emerald waters of Shasta Lake's McCloud River Arm are capped by the 3114-foot-high North Gray Rocks, a sight so awesome you'll be turning your gaze to it often. The renowned Shasta Caverns are nestled beneath this deep gray mountain. These massive gray outcroppings are composed of limestone, which are compressed skeletal remnants of animals that lived over 200 million years ago.

Take the Shasta Caverns Road exit off I-5, some 15 miles north of Redding. After driving east 0.4 mile, turn right onto Bailey Cove Road, drive 0.7 mile until the road ends, and pick up the trailhead near the water's edge (signed Bailey Cove Loop). The trail begins in a clockwise direction a few yards past a huge canyon live oak and beneath some juvenile ponderosa pine.

The mostly flat footpath lingers enticingly close above Shasta Lake's edge and swings southward out of the cove through colonies of tall whiteleaf manzanita. Mainly low-growing poison oak creeps along the few sunny spots at the start of the trip (count how many poison oak vines are creeping up ponderosa pines or black oaks). Watch closely for clear views to the east of the lake's expansive waters reflecting the sculpted rocky cliff face of North Gray Rocks. At 1.3 miles the trail heads underneath a scattered grove of tall and lean knobcone pines and reaches a gulch offering easy access to a small cove. Pass a collection of common mullein plants with large gray fans as leaves to reach this ideal spot for picnicking, photography, and swimming.

Other secluded lakeside perches follow along the orange and rocky shoreline, some decorated with patches of spring-flowering blue lupines. Linger long in these cozy, quiet, and secluded coves, for at 1.8 miles sounds of I-5 traffic coincide with the distant sight of moving vehicles.

A cluster of buckeye trees next to a seasonal stream hugs the trailside, nestled beneath an open forest of towering black oak trees. Soon after, look for a patch of bush poppy (yellow flowers in spring) on both sides of the trail. The final mile loops above a larger cove (Johns Creek inlet) and sunnier sections than Bailey Cove. Here, the canyon live oaks grow mainly as large, squat shrubs amidst occasional ceanothus and redbud.

If time and energy permit, climb the unsigned trail on the right at journey's end. Toward the top, the way gets tough to negotiate, requiring a bit of bushwhacking. Salvage some views between black oaks and gray pines.

11   CLIKAPUDI BAY AND CREEK

Distance: 6.8-mile loop; 4.2 miles round trip to Clikapudi Bay
Difficulty: Moderate
High point: 1300 feet
Elevation gain: 700 feet
Map: USGS Millville
Nearest campground: Jones Valley Campground, phone (530) 275-1589
Information: Shasta Lake Ranger District, Shasta-Trinity National
    Forest, phone (530) 275-1589

Here's an ultimate off-season hike with memorable views of Shasta Lake that explores the lake's curving shoreline, offering seclusion, a well-made trail, visits to Wintu Indian archaeological sites, and splendid samples of numerous native foothill trees and shrubs. The trip is mostly shaded during warm late spring or early fall days. A field of lupine blooms profusely in midspring, and you'll encounter intimate streams galore in winter and early spring. In fact, plan on stepping with delight over these cute little lake inlets an average of once every 0.3 mile. Share the trail with fishermen and mountain bikers.

From I-5 in north Redding, take Highway 299 east and drive about 6 miles to Bella Vista. Turn north on Dry Creek Road and drive 6.8

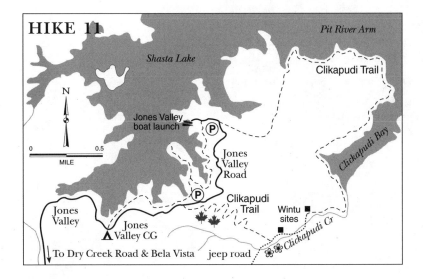

HIKE 11

Pit River Arm

Shasta Lake

Clikapudi Trail

N

0   0.5
MILE

Jones Valley
boat launch

 P

Jones
Valley
Road

P

Clikapudi
Trail

Clikapudi Bay

Wintu
sites

Jones
Valley

Jones
▲ Valley CG

↓ To Dry Creek Road & Bela Vista   jeep road

Clikapudi Cr

miles to the Y with Jones Valley Road. Go right on it, drive 1.2 miles,
and park in the small gravel lot on the left side just past the yellow 25
mph sign. The trail starts next to the sign.

At the get go, the yard-wide dirt footpath that is Clikapudi Trail
climbs a hillside for 0.4 mile in an open woodland of black oaks, ponderosa pines, gray pines (higher up), and massive whiteleaf manzanitas.
It then promptly leads down to and lingers in a narrow slot, staying
intimately close to a slender seasonal stream that slithers from late
autumn into midspring. This U-shaped valley is peacefully enlighten-
ing, with abundant moss thriving on many of the older interior live
oaks, deciduous oaks, and manzanitas.

At 0.9 mile, go left as the trail temporarily joins a dirt jeep road.
There is a sign on a fence post indicating a sacred Wintu Indian site,
which consists of ancient ruins, fossils, and historical remnants (all
protected). You'll soon cross modest Clikapudi Creek, bear left on a
slender footpath, duck underneath a dual-trunked valley oak giant,
and reach the second fragile and irreplaceable Wintu Indian site at
1.2 miles.

After 0.5 mile of looking down on Clikapudi Creek, note how it
suddenly gets faster, bigger, steeper, and rockier as it climaxes into
Clikapudi Bay. There's a nice spot here past driftwood and alongside
a small grove of willows to soak, sooth, and cool your active feet at the
union of creek with bay.

A wooden bridge crosses a quiet, driftwood-strewn inlet creek of

Clikapudi Creek, midwinter

the bay at 2.2 miles. The placid gray waters of Clikapudi Bay widen perceptively at the third feeder stream crossing at 2.7 miles, where you will see plenty of wild California grape. Water slides over pure rock at the fourth and fifth stream crossings, signaling a slight transformation in soil profile and native vegetation.

Shrubby forms of canyon live oak accompany some tall and dense clusters of whiteleaf manzanita before the trail veers abruptly at a vista overlooking a pair of peninsulas highlighting a curvaceous stretch of Shasta Lake at 3.6 miles (Pit River Arm). A lone, proud, and youthful ponderosa pine stands guard atop the closest peninsula. At 3.8 miles, take a moment to appreciate a handsome, 20-foot-tall madrone on the trail's left side next to a moss-covered black oak giant. From here a spur trail leads directly to a small peninsula—when the lake level is low enough, which is most of the time, this is an ideal winter spot for admiring a snowcapped Cascade Range section to the east.

As the trail swings around a driftwood-lined inlet stream at 4.2 miles, gaze skyward at tall and slender knobcone pines—they intersperse the Douglas firs and ponderosa pines for the remainder of the trip. As the trail continues to hug the shore, watch for styrax shrubs (white flowers in May) and blue flowered ceanothus shrubs (also in May).

At 5 miles, after passing some coffeeberry shrubs at the union of two seasonal creeks, the trail climbs out of the canyon, down along a cove, and then up to the Jones Valley boat launch parking lot at 5.8 miles. Continue on the trail as it resumes after the parking lot, pass a couple of coves with views and return to your car.

12 ⚘ HIRZ BAY TRAIL

Distance: 4 miles round trip
Difficulty: Easy to moderate
High point: 1200 feet
Elevation gain: 700 feet
Maps: USGS Bollibokka Mountain, Lamoine
Nearest campground: Hirz Bay Campground, phone (530) 275-1589 or (530) 275-1587
Information: Shasta Lake Ranger District, Shasta-Trinity National Forest, phone (530) 275-1587

Get intimate with the sloping shoreline of Shasta Lake, California's largest reservoir. By exploring three small creeks where they finish in cozy coves, a hiker can stroll 2 precious miles of Shasta Lake's 370-mile-long shoreline, which exceeds that of San Francisco Bay. Watch for fellow hikers with fishing poles strapped to their day packs.

This hike features seventeen native trees, shrubs, and vines described below, and shows off several outcrops of limestone, the compressed-into-rock remains of marine animals deposited some 200 million years ago on ancient seabeds. The bigleaf maples, dogwoods, and Fremont cottonwoods nestled along the creeks provide flashes of yellow and red in autumn, while the black oaks scattered along the slopes furnish unique orange and brown hues. The creeks along this hike get enchantingly urgent in late winter and early spring, when there is also occasional snow atop the Klamath Mountains that surround the lake.

From I-5 some 20 miles north of Redding, take signed Gilman Road. Follow this scenic and paved road east for 10.2 miles, and then park at the signed Dekkas Rock Picnic Area.

Views of Shasta Lake's McCloud River Arm are frequent from the moment you leave the trailhead on the west side of the Dekkas Rock Picnic Area until you reach campsite 46 at Hirz Bay, the turnaround point. You can also arrange for a car to meet you at the Hirz Bay Campground to shorten the hike. A glorious outlook on Shasta Lake

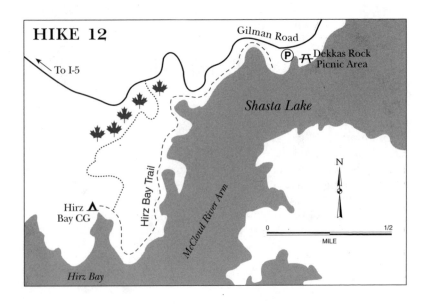

HIKE 12

Gilman Road

To I-5

Dekkas Rock Picnic Area

Shasta Lake

Hirz Bay Trail

McCloud River Arm

Hirz Bay CG

N

0   1/2
MILE

Hirz Bay

McCloud River Arm from Hirz Bay spur trail

greets you from the get go, showing off a pair of bumpy mountain tops beyond a large, leaning, and moss-covered canyon live oak. The sloping dirt foot trail promptly descends to a crossing of a live-oak-lined narrow stream and a well-built wooden bridge. From here you can traipse past a driftwood pile for easy access to a cove for fishing and/or sightseeing.

The trail then gets rocky over a short climbing spur past buckeyes, black oaks, and some precariously leaning gray pines. A handful of redbuds, ferns, and wild California grape decorate the trailside at 0.4 mile, where driftwood and cottonwoods highlight a pretty view of a small cove along this finger of the McCloud River Arm.

The trail climbs in canyon oak woodland with scattered ponderosa pines, then straightens at a cluster of whiteleaf manzanita at 0.7 mile. It then drops to an unsigned Y-junction where a spur trail continues straight and the main trail veers sharply right (make note of this for return trip). Take this delightful 0.4 mile round-trip spur trail past a standout, triple-trunked canyon live oak overlooking a slim and nicely shaped cove. Proceed beyond an eroded gully, a perch of gray limestone boulders with great views of the lake, and arrive at an eastward view of a limestone-boulder-capped hill.

Back on the main trail, having walked 1.2 miles, you promptly reach a wooden bridge that crosses a gorgeous skinny stream toppling gracefully over limestone boulders and scattered driftwood into the aforementioned cove. Dogwoods, bigleaf maples, white alders, buckeyes, and Douglas firs shade a bench overlooking the scene.

The trail then swings along a slope highlighted by knobcone pines and crosses a gulch near a cove. At 2.1 miles, notice the ground cover of California honeysuckle at a stream laden with sword ferns next to a wooden bridge. Reach ponderosa pine inundated Hirz Bay Campground 0.1 mile farther. Picnic here, and then retrace your steps to enjoy a variety of lake views from different vantage points. Alternately, arrange to have a second car waiting at the campground to drive you back to the trailhead parking area.

13 ♣ WATERS GULCH CREEK TO PACKERS BAY

Distance: 6.8-mile loop
Difficulty: Moderate
High point: 1500 feet
Elevation gain: 1100 feet
Map: USGS O'Brien
Nearest campground: Bailey Cove Campground, phone (530) 275-1587
Information: Shasta Lake Ranger District, Shasta-Trinity National
　　　Forest, phone (530) 275-1589

See Hike 13 map on p. 44.

The coves and surrounding mountainsides of Shasta Lake's Sacramento River Arm appear extra special when viewed from this hike's several vantage points. Check out these scenes at sunrise or twilight and they can seem surreal. A portion of the trip explores attractively skinny Waters Gulch Creek, featuring a little waterfall that loses intensity in the summer until heavy rains return in the fall. Catch it in spring when it's swift and experience the bonus of adjoining cascades crashing suddenly into still lake water. You'll wander into a black oak metropolis that transforms into a perpetual wave of lemon orange by late October. California's most colorful deciduous oak tree is arguably the most bountiful on this hike than on any other. The recently discovered Shasta snow wreath, a rose family shrub, can also be found along this hike.

Shasta Dam, spring

Some 15 miles north of Redding on I-5, 3 miles past the bridge over Shasta Lake, take the Packers Bay exit (it's also signed for Shasta Caverns). Drive beneath the freeway, get on I-5 south, and take the Packers Bay exit 1 mile farther. Turn right, travel 1 mile, and turn right into the small paved parking lot.

To start, take the short climb on the slender Overlook Trail, which serves as a quadriceps/lung warm-up and culminates in a rewarding and secluded vista of the Central Valley Water Project's mainstay—Shasta Lake. Black oaks canopy poison oak, styrax bushes (white flowers in May and June), ceanothus (blue flowers in May), currant, and yellow-flowered mules ears. An old rotted log resting on rock piles offers a westward view of the top of Shasta Bally and a handful of Shasta Lake's remote minicoves. A hop and a skip higher puts you at a site overlooking Packers Bay. Awkwardly twisted gray pines offer virtually no shade, allowing the buckbrush and large whiteleaf manzanita to partially block the views.

After descending this mostly shaded 0.4-mile-long trail, go down the signed Waters Gulch Trail, which promptly leads to its namesake creek. Douglas fir thrive on this moister north facing slope, casting dark shadows in spots. A steep but negotiable spur trail soon leads past a stand of fragrant California bay laurel trees and to the crown of a small but powerfully gushing waterfall. To reach the place where the falls exit into a clear pool followed by cascades, head down the main trail about 100 yards. Proceed cautiously down a short side trail where a seasonal stream on the other shore topples gracefully into the creek's mouth and the lake's finger. If the lake is full, which is rare, you'll have to swim 20 yards in comparatively warm lake water to reach this noisy setting. Go ahead and soothe your back muscles with the jets in the whirlpool created by the small falls. Large and flat boulder slabs offer prime picnicking and sun-worshipping perches.

The trail leaves behind the dogwoods, alders, bigleaf maples, and a patch of elephant ears thriving in the whirlpool. The scene switches to a tranquil, intimate setting, tracing the wooded shoreline of a large cove. Wood planks cross lazy streams that meander into driftwood-laden cove slots. It's easy to get lost in a daydream here when filtered sunlight strikes pleasing patterns on the bracken ferns and other ground cover greenery at trailside.

At 2.2 miles, look for the solitary, tiny island just offshore, dominated by a flat-topped ponderosa pine guarding a handful of manzanita shrubs. The trail then climbs inland under the occasional shade of black oaks to a knoll and a wooden bench at 2.7 miles. Lake views now vanish on this flat ridge section, replaced by the steep south and west facing slopes, densely clothed in a mosaic of chaparral streaked with gray pines and swirls of canyon live oaks. The trail then meets a polite stream at 3.2 miles and briefly follows it to a thicket of wild mock orange shrubs.

You soon cross another brook beside the often overgrown but signed Fish Loop Trail. Used mainly by fishermen, this 0.5-mile, flat trail pales in comparison to the Waters Gulch Trail, with mediocre views of the docked Packers Bay houseboats. You can turn around here and retrace your steps, or walk a few paces farther to the access road next to the marina and climb 0.5 mile to the car.

14 ❦ SACRAMENTO RIVER TO KESWICK DAM

Distance: 5.2 miles round trip; 3 miles round trip to the big footbridge
Difficulty: Easy
High point: 600 feet
Elevation gain: 300 feet
Map: USGS Redding
Nearest campground: Oak Bottom Campground, phone (530) 246-1225
Information: City of Redding Parks Department, phone (530) 224-6100

I've canoed several sections of the Sacramento River and discovered the stretch along this hike is perhaps the most rugged, wild, and scenic of them all. It's a paradox that the well-planned Sacramento River Trail is so closely surrounded by the city of Redding, yet retains a sense of remoteness and natural beauty.

Take a camera on this hike, which reveals an interesting contrast between dry and sunny areas on the northeast banks of the icy cold

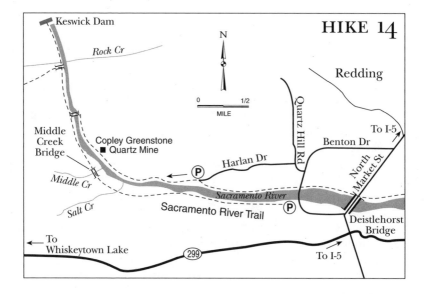

Sacramento River and occasionally riparian, shady, and noticeably moister southwest banks. There's a tremendous view of a gorgeous stretch of river fronting Lassen Peak and Chaos Crags—watch for it on your return, 0.5 mile from the trailhead. All winter long, this trail displays these peaks glistening in snow, along with Shasta Bally. Several creeks and tributaries along the route look their best when full and fast in winter and early spring. The best time to achieve some solitude is on autumn weekdays and rainy days. Mountain bikers also use this trail.

From I-5 in Redding, take Highway 299 west and follow all signs indicating North 273 (which is North Market Street). Turn right on North Market Street and then turn left (west) on Quartz Hill Road and drive 0.8 mile, crossing the Sacramento River. Go left on paved Harlan Drive, travel 1 mile, and park at the road's end next to a large redwood grove.

Go right on the Sacramento River Trail. The wide, paved path reaches a colony of large, lichen-coated boulders at 0.3 mile, which have been etched into the riverbanks by centuries of flooding. These boulders of igneous volcanic bedrock are composed mainly of gabbro and, along with a natural barrier of ceanothus shrubs, decorate this calm but swirling stretch of river. Continue in blue oak woodland and dry chaparral past several interpretive signs and three bench vistas to a fourth bench at 0.7 mile offering a better view of a swifter portion of the river. The view of Shasta Bally and South Fork Mountain to the west looks its most splendid just past the transmitter lines alongside a handsome and youthful gray pine at 0.9 mile.

Interior live oak tends to take over for a ways, interspersed with whiteleaf manzanita and toyon shrubs (red berries in early winter). A small and attractive tributary trickles past ferns, where a bench next to a unique knobcone pine overlooks a craggy solid rock island perched in the river. Reach the Copley Greenstone Quartz Mine 100 yards farther, which is composed of old lava flows and river sediments altered by heat and pressure over the last several hundred million years. The river's current is blocked by another rock island at 1.3 miles, forming surging rapids and an undercurrent.

Reach the impressive 13-foot-wide footbridge at 1.5 miles, specially built in 1990. Go ahead and spit and watch it vanish into the smooth flowing river some 30 feet below. The riverbanks here are decorated by a colorful mosaic of irregularly shaped angular large boulders. Cross the bridge and proceed right on a wide cinder trail. As you approach Keswick Dam (visible in the distance), note how the river narrows—it was an ideal spot for the Waugh's Ferry to transport miners across the river on their way to the town of Buckeye. Speaking of which, look for native deciduous buckeye trees (white flower spikes in May) nestled in the mossy rock cliffs on the trail's west side.

Reach magnificent and fittingly named Rock Creek at 1.8 miles, and watch it empty into the river just downstream from Keswick Dam. Turn around here and traipse 75 yards to an old fashioned rock and railroad-tie bridge that you passed. Follow a slender foot trail west as

Sacramento River and manzanita growing out of rock, winter

it traces a seasonal creek that usually flows from December through April. The blue oak, live oak, manzanita, and occasional toyon, coffeeberry, and willow thriving in this U-shaped canyon can best be appreciated over the first 0.25 mile.

If you have leftover energy and curiosity, continue straight when you reach the big footbridge again at 2.7 miles. The scenes of the river from the southeast side are as impressive as those from the other side, at least for the first 0.5 mile. Ordinary looking Middle Creek Bridge at 3.2 miles is supported by hand-carved sandstone, and over a century ago was a route for ore-bearing cars of the Central Pacific Railroad. To continue further to the parking area off Benton Drive is to pass old run-down structures, groves of exotic ailanthus and black locust trees, and plenty of powerlines, in-line skaters, and friendly families—you can keep the wilderness experience intact by retracing your steps from here.

15 ⚘ BOULDER CREEK FALLS AND MILL CREEK

Distance: 6.2 miles one-way to Mill Creek; 4.8 miles round trip to Boulder Creek Falls
Difficulty: Moderate
High point: 2250 feet
Elevation gain: 1000 feet
Map: USGS French Gulch
Nearest campground: Oak Bottom Campground, phone (530) 241-6584
Information: Whiskeytown Unit, Whiskeytown-Shasta-Trinity National Recreation Area, phone (530) 246-1225 or (530) 242-3400

Arguably the most impressive waterfall near Whiskeytown Lake, 120-foot-long Boulder Creek Falls is a nice surprise. Combine it with the spring-flowering dogwoods along lush and mystic Mill Creek, and this hike is a double delight. The vibrant colors of the bigleaf maples and dogwoods are enticing during midautumn, when the falls are half as intense. By late winter and early spring, the falls are fast, loud, powerful, and white. Plan on getting wet while crossing Boulder Creek four times and Mill Creek nineteen times. The Mill Creek Trail, a nature lover's paradise with deep shade and large granite boulders, fades in spots. Stay alert and look for ribbons tied to trees and you should be fine. Arrange for a car to meet you at the Mill Creek parking area if you choose the one-way route.

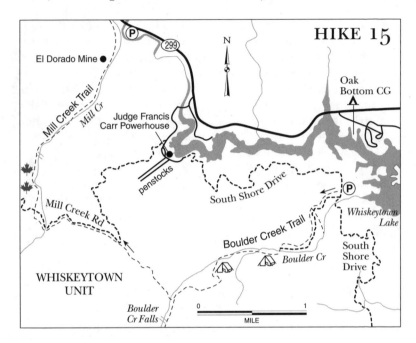

Drive Highway 299 2 miles northwest from the turnoff for Oak Bottom Campground and turn left on Judge Francis Carr Powerhouse Road. After 0.3 mile past the powerhouse, the road turns into dirt South Shore Drive. Reach a crossroads in 2.3 miles and park. The trailhead is beyond the gate. If you plan a car shuttle for this hike, the Mill Creek parking lot is on the south side of Highway 299, just east of the bridge across Clear Creek, 1.3 miles beyond the Carr Powerhouse Road turnoff.

Your trail, a rocky old dirt road, at first climbs gently past whiteleaf manzanita, ponderosa pine, black oak, toyon, and ceanothus. At 0.4 mile, a spur trail darts left and promptly leads to an old mine overlooking scenic Boulder Creek. Shasta Bally, usually snowcapped through April, looms ahead beyond canyon live oaks as you reach the union of Boulder Creek with a seasonal stream at 0.8 mile. Youthful Douglas firs show up as the mellow climb continues 1 mile to the first crossing of Boulder Creek beneath a colony of slender white alders.

Soon pass the first trailside campsite. Then reach two sugar pines—by far the largest conifers so far on the hike—25 yards before the creek's second crossing. The trail veers away from the creek after the third crossing, reaching a second campsite and gently ascending in continued partial shade past the remains of an old homestead. Shasta Bally looms close just before descending to the final crossing of Boulder Creek at 2.3 miles. Follow the scant trail left along the east side of the creek as it climbs 100 feet in elevation to tall and slender Boulder Creek Falls.

Adorned by the occasional bigleaf maple, Boulder Creek Falls are a triple-decker masterpiece. The highest falls cascade into the middle falls, which plummet into a pool surrounded by mossy rocks. From here, you can watch the lower falls plunge some 75 feet into a sand-bottomed clear pool. Retrace your steps from Boulder Creek Falls for the shorter trip.

Boulder Creek Trail stays wide and becomes littered with pine needles as it continues across the creek, where it stays mostly level over the next 0.6 mile in serene forest. Eventually the trail descends to a three-way junction at 3.5 miles, next to knobcone pines and manzanita clusters. Bear left onto Mill Creek Road. After 0.6 mile mostly downhill, the well-graded dirt road crosses Mill Creek and soon reaches Mill Creek Trail, where you go right.

The dirt road becomes a narrower trail and then steeply descends a ridge before following Mill Creek for awhile. The hillside to the left is awash in fall color in October. Notice the waterfall a bit farther if you make the trip in the spring. You soon cross Mill Creek and walk under plentiful dogwoods for a couple hundred yards before reaching a 5-foot-long waterfall that topples into a nice swimming hole. Watch for a huge incense cedar farther on, and then some California wild grape vines draping over countless ponderosa pines. Reach the interesting El Dorado Mine at 6.1 miles. The Mill Creek parking lot is just another 0.1 mile.

Boulder Creek Falls, late winter

16 ⚘ DAVIS GULCH TRAIL AND WHISKEYTOWN LAKE

Distance: 6.8 miles round trip; 3.6 miles round trip to ridge
Difficulty: Moderate
High point: 1500 feet
Elevation gain: 600 feet
Map: USGS French Gulch
Nearest campground: Oak Bottom Campground, phone (530) 241-6584
Information: Whiskeytown Unit, Whiskeytown-Shasta-Trinity National
    Recreation Area, phone (530) 246-1225 or (530) 242-3400

Numerous little gulches are the main allure of this trip, especially after a good rainy spell in winter or early spring when they are in their prime. The tranquil flow of a gin-clear low mountain stream gurgling over little boulder tapestries is a soothing symphony to your ears and attracts fishermen. Each gulch encompasses its special traits, with miniature cascades (winter and early spring), mossy rock cliffs and tree trunks, and a bounty of lush green native plants landscaped by nature.

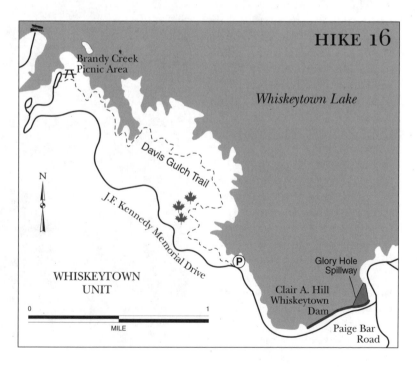

Whiskeytown Lake from Davis Gulch Trail, winter

This hike features an impressive plethora of thriving native plant species. Besides those detailed below, look for sword fern, buckeye (near mine shaft), mountain mahogany (near ridge), interior live oak, poison oak, yerba santa, wild blackberry and California grape (in some gulches), incense cedar and Douglas fir (near trailhead), and white alder (in first big gulch).

From the historic park in Shasta, drive 2 miles west along Highway 299 to the Whiskeytown Lake Visitor Information Center and turn left onto J.F. Kennedy Memorial Drive. Drive 1.6 miles and follow the road right past the Glory Hole Spillway. The trailhead is on the right 1.1 mile farther.

Just 25 yards down the clay-packed Davis Gulch Trail, a short spur trail on the right drops 100 feet in elevation to twin cozy coves. This secluded site offers good bass fishing and can be saved until journey's end for a dip on a warm early autumn day, when the water is still comfortable.

Back on Davis Gulch Trail, a mostly shaded, wide dirt path, wander past a couple of serene gulches to a larger gulch at 0.3 mile featuring one of this hike's twenty interpretive signs—this one for canyon live oak. The real highlight here is the neighboring canyon live oak on the left with large roots attempting to bust through lichen-covered boulders anchored in the soil.

If it's late autumn through winter, delight in the crunch of your footsteps landing on large bigleaf maple and black oak leaves, canyon live oak acorns, and the occasional ponderosa pine cone or ashy coal twig debris from tall whiteleaf manzanita. Note how the evergreen toyon shrubs are alive and well on these mostly east and north facing canyon slopes. A throng of seedlings and saplings are scattered amid 10-foot-tall toyons, decorated with red berries around Christmastime.

Climb to a thicket of shrub-form Brewer oak at 1.4 miles. An interpretive sign indicates the high efficiency of this spreading variety of Oregon oak for preventing soil erosion. One of Davis Gulch Trail's twelve benches is located here, showing off a striking scene of deep gray blue Whiskeytown Lake to the east, punctuated by a grove of knobcone pines.

Ascend an exposed ridge at 1.8 miles, densely clothed in whiteleaf manzanita. Rub the pleasingly fragrant gray leaves of the ground sage and look for the miniature needles of the chamise shrub as well as some sporadic, leaning gray pines. A gorgeous and curvaceous cove at 2.1 miles shows off a pair of tiny islands in the distance. At 2.4 miles, reach an old mining cave that's been filled in with dirt on the other side of the cove. The final mile to Brandy Creek Picnic Area displays open scenes of the lake to the old boat launching area just east of Brandy Creek Beach. Walk through the picnic area to hang out at the beach and then return as you came.

17 ⚘ KANAKA PEAK

Distance: 7.8-mile loop
Difficulty: Strenuous
High point: 2700 feet
Elevation gain: 1900 feet
Map: USGS French Gulch
Nearest campground: Peltier Valley Campground, phone (530) 242-3400
Information: Whiskeytown Unit, Whiskeytown-Shasta-Trinity National Recreation Area, phone (530) 246-1225 or (530) 242-3400

When the Wintu Indians went hunting on Kanaka Peak with bow and arrow long ago, they admired a different view than what you'll see on this hike. They saw the flooding Sacramento River where Redding and Anderson now lie. They saw a blanket of open forest where recreational Whiskeytown Lake now sprawls. Gorgeous Paige Boulder Creek, which you cross several times on this hike, was a solid fishing source for the Wintu Indians. Several of the gullies and dug trenches you'll see on this hike were mined for gold by white settlers, whose incursion precipitated the rapid decline of the Wintu.

Hike here in late winter and early spring and adore a waterfall and several cascades roaring down Paige Boulder Creek. Frequent snow on the surrounding Klamath Mountain tops is another bonus. The benefits of autumn hiking include viewing the vibrant colors of bigleaf maple, black oak, and dogwood leaves and toyon berries. Mountain bikers and horseback riders also use this trail.

From the historic park in Shasta, drive west 2 miles along Highway 299 to J.F. Kennedy Memorial Drive. Turn left, drive about 2 miles to the Glory Hole Spillway, and turn left (south) onto Paige Bar Road. After 1 mile, turn right onto dirt Peltier Valley Road. The dirt road

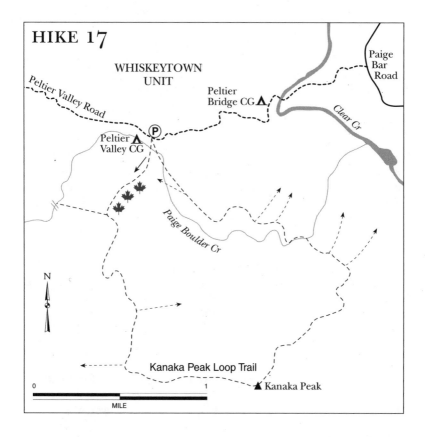

HIKE 17

WHISKEYTOWN UNIT

Peltier Valley Road

Paige Bar Road

Peltier Bridge CG ▲

Clear Cr

Ⓟ

Peltier ▲ Valley CG

Paige Boulder Cr

N

Kanaka Peak Loop Trail

▲ Kanaka Peak

0   1

MILE

crosses a bridge, goes up for 1.7 miles, and then crosses a seasonal stream. Park in the clearing. To start, cross Paige Boulder Creek via huge granite boulders, and turn right on the unsigned Kanaka Peak Loop Trail. It follows the crystal clear stream for about 100 yards and then veers upward as the trail widens beneath ponderosa pine and occasional black oak and canyon live oak. During the climb, the trail alternates between full shade of bigleaf maples near the moist gulches, scattered shade in occasional buckeye groves, and sunny sites with chaparral of whiteleaf manzanita and some toyon. Visit in the fall for a spectacular color show.

Look closely for a slimmer side trail on the right at 1 mile in a flat area. This is one of several side trails along the loop that can extend this hike if you have the time. This side trail heads into dense woods and 0.4 mile farther reaches a slender waterfall that crashes 15 feet over solid granite. Several room-sized boulder outcrops furnish ideal perches for admiring this wild and rocky stretch of Paige Boulder Creek. When the creek is raging in late winter and early spring, it's a mix of small cascades culminating in sand-bottomed pools.

Retrace your steps and continue on the Kanaka Peak Loop Trail and reach a view of Kanaka Peak in 0.2 mile. After another 0.3 mile, cross a stream beneath a leaning and towering canyon live oak. The narrow stream of water here cascades gently over a moss-covered rock face. The trail soon climbs steeply, and eventually reaches a ridge with a view past black oaks of Whiskeytown Lake. A superb, multitrunked, leaning canyon live oak towers over a Whiskeytown Unit boundary sign here. The trail then descends steeply but briefly, climbing again another 0.3 mile to Kanaka Peak with well-deserved views north and south to ease the effort. A solitary sugar pine (look for the foot-long cones on the ground) indicates you're close to the top.

To obtain a panorama, scurry around the manzanita and large canyon live oak shrubs. The top portion of Mount Shasta peaks over the Klamath Mountains and Whiskeytown Lake to the north. The bumpy Trinity Alps glisten with snow to the northwest. Spy the radio towers atop Shasta Bally to the west. The smooth Yolla Bolly Mountains hover over the bald hills of Platina to the south. Look over the Mule Mountain Range to Redding in the east. Miles of the Cascade Range are on view, highlighted by Lassen Peak punctuating the Upper Sacramento Valley.

The trail plunges dramatically down a once charred but recovering area of the 1991 Kanaka Peak fire. The views are mainly of the lake past ponderosa pines and a ceanothus ground cover. After 1 mile the steepness lessens as you drop into a forest shaded by Douglas fir. Boulder-hop Paige Boulder Creek, featuring a cluster of juvenile incense cedars on the other shore. The trail climbs upslope for awhile, displaying a rugged Kanaka Peak standing guard over a wild stretch of the creek. The trail then descends to follow near creekside to the trailhead.

Upper Sacramento Valley from Kanaka Peak

CHICO VICINITY

18 ⚑ HOG LAKE TO PAYNES CREEK

Distance: 7.6 miles round trip
Difficulty: Easy
High point: 700 feet
Elevation gain: 400 feet
Map: Bureau of Land Management map
Nearest campground: Battle Creek Campground, phone (530) 258-2141
Information: Bureau of Land Management, (530) 224-2100

This hike is rich in local history, traipsing across a plain where the Yahi Indians tribes roamed and elk and antelope grazed. Official Ishi country is a few flaps of the hawk's wings to the south. A typical hike in reverse, this journey leaves a small lake and heads down to big ol' Paynes Creek, past abundant spring flowering wildflowers and far-reaching views to the east and west that are spectacular when the mountains are snow clad (usually December into May). The easy and short cross-country scamper across Hog Lake Plateau to Hog Lake is enticing, where various boulder perches provide grand views of the Cascade Range and Yolla Bolly Mountains.

Mount Shasta stands guard over a rim of blue oaks above Hog

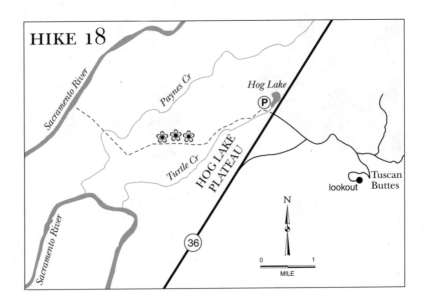

Hog Lake, early spring

Lake to the north. The lake offers a scene of Snow and Clover Mountains in the Cascades, with Black Butte in the foreground. Scanning clockwise, look for Magee and Crater Peaks and finally Lassen Peak glowing above Inskip Hill and the lake. Marshy Hog Lake (chances are your boots will get wet and muddy getting there) is frequently patrolled by egrets and geese before it dries up in summer. Expect to encounter horseback riders and mountain bikers along this trail.

From I-5 in Red Bluff, 30 miles south of Redding, take the Highway 36 East exit and follow all signs for Lassen Park. From the junction of Highways 99 and 36, turn east onto Highway 36 and continue 7.3 miles to the small gravel parking lot in front of Hog Lake, on the left side of the highway.

The nonmotorized trail, an old cattle dirt road, at first slices across the northern boundary of Hog Lake Plateau, with old blue oaks scattered among basalt outcrops adorning the hillside landscape. There are sweeping vistas across the plain of earlier described mountains behind and ahead of you. The wide trail swerves northwesterly at 1.7 miles, revealing an impressive inaugural view into the fertile Upper Sacramento Valley. A couple hundred yards farther, Bully Choop Mountain, Shasta Bally Mountain, and the jagged Trinity Alps (in the Klamath Mountains) appear suddenly. Soon after that, the Trinity Divide, just west of the town of Mount Shasta, rises beyond a picturesque scene of shapely blue oaks and wildflowers in spring. Then there's an encore presentation of Mount Shasta. These natural monuments continue to inspire as the trail now descends gently and quickly under transmitter lines (note the bald eagle's nest at the top) at 2.6 miles.

At 3.8 miles the wide, dual-channeled section of Paynes Creek appears in front of a green valley and marsh. Redbud and elderberry bushes are strewn in the basaltic boulder banks on the other shore, while willows and western sycamore trees dot the sandy pocket beaches and rounded sedimentary rock strips along Paynes Creek's flood zone. Wild California grape climb powerfully up many of the trees. The creek races swifter than the typical flow of the Sacramento River, which meanders just past the marshland to the west.

19 ⚜ NORTH FORK ANTELOPE CREEK

Distance: 12.6 miles round trip
Difficulty: Moderate; the final 2-mile climb is strenuous
High point: 2740 feet
Elevation gain: 1900 feet
Maps: USGS Finley Butte, Panther Spring
Nearest campground: Battle Creek Campground, phone (530) 258-2141
Information: Almanor Ranger District, Lassen National Forest,
    phone (530) 258-2141

The scenery here harkens back to a typical sprawling outdoor scene in a western movie. Several elements combine to conjure a frontier feel: grassy patches next to clusters of gray conifers and shrubs; far-reaching views of mighty mountains in the distance and, nearby, hogback ridges

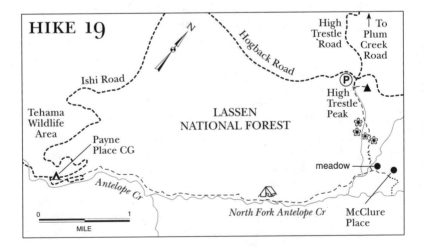

Antelope Creek Canyon, late winter

(long, flat, and extensive ridge lines resembling a hog's back); exposed pockets of wildflowers in spring; boulders buffeted by a crashing creek; and horses that share the trail. This is the land where Ishi and other Yahi Yana Indians roamed over bizarre basaltic rock outcroppings and other lichen-coated lava rocks. In fact, Ishi Wilderness is a mere few miles as the bald eagle flies to the south.

From Red Bluff, drive Highway 36 east about 20 miles to Paynes Creek and turn right on Paynes Creek Road. After just 0.3 mile, turn right onto paved Plum Creek Road and go 5.2 miles. Turn right onto dirt High Trestle Road, drive 2.5 miles, and park in the dirt area just past Hogback Road.

As a warm-up, climb High Trestle Peak to the east of your parked car through a mixed woodland of mainly blue oak with some interior live oak and black oak. Scramble atop various lava boulders embedded on this peak, which is 0.25 mile away. Snag a unique panorama past stubby blue oaks and a couple of buckeyes and huge and handsome greenleaf manzanitas. On a clear winter's day, look north to spy Mounts Shasta and Lassen, and Magee Peaks, as well as various peaks in the Klamath Mountains, such as the Trinities.

For the first 2 miles toward North Fork Antelope Creek, the trail is briefly an abandoned dirt road, and then a footpath that snakes gently down a sunny canyonside. Take in breathtaking views of chaparral and squat oak-clad Antelope Creek Canyon. A modest and graceful feeder stream at 0.6 mile accompanies the first part of this stretch past profuse native wildflowers in spring (blue lupine and brodiaea and white popcornlike flowers), buckbrush ceanothus, canyon live oaks in bush form, and lush and healthy gray pines.

71

At 1.8 miles, toward the bottom of the hill, the trail crosses another gulch and proceeds into a narrow meadow laced with buttercups in spring. Take the spur trail on the left, which wanders farther down the meadow and soon to McClure Place, once a ranch, where fences and rock structures still stand.

Back on the main trail, recross the previously mentioned feeder streams, and stay above and within earshot of North Fork Antelope Creek. Roaring incessantly, this creek dashes madly, invigorated by numerous springs and side streams cutting through gulches. After walking cautiously past a couple of springs and a trail section laden with poison oak, watch for a few rare California nutmeg conifers.

The first creekside campsite is perched on a flat at 3.2 miles, yielding a close-up view down on North Fork Antelope Creek. Partially shaded by canyon live oak, buckeyes, and blue oaks, this spot features California wild grape (note the thick, ropelike trunks) and some tall ponderosa pine specimens across the bank.

The rest of the journey proceeds along the banks of the alder-bordered creek to the confluence of the north and south forks of Antelope Creek at 4.9 miles. Finish at the boundary of the Tehama Wildlife Area.

20 ❦ ORLAND BUTTES

Distance: Up to 6 miles round trip
Difficulty: Easy to moderate
High point: 200 feet
Elevation gain: 300 feet
Map: USGS Flournoy
Nearest campground: Buckhorn Campground, phone (530) 865-4781
Information: Black Butte Lake District, U.S. Army Corps of Engineers, phone (530) 865-4781

The low but steep Orland Buttes punctuate flatlands that surround Orland, hiding scenic Black Butte Lake and offering awesome views from their summits. Black Butte Lake, fed by Stony Creek, is a popular fishing spot. The lake was named for the prominent geological rock cliff formations near Eagle Pass called the Orland Buttes. These buttes were formed by an extensive lava flow occurring millions of years ago that poured from the vicinity of Chico.

Take this hike on a clear day from December through April and

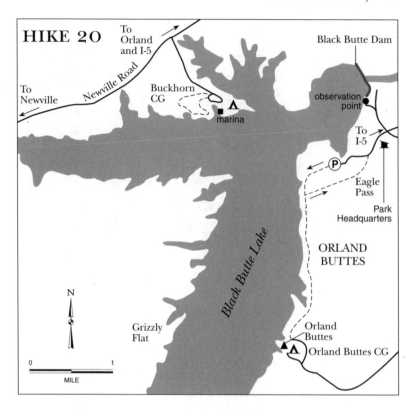

be rewarded with countless photogenic vistas displaying snowcapped mountains beyond rolling green hills in all directions. Bird enthusiasts can also have a field day on this excursion (pick up the bird brochure from park headquarters). Red-tailed hawks are commonly seen patrolling the buttes for mice and squirrels while turkey vultures roam lower, looking for dead animals. Flickers linger near the oaks while great blue herons cruise over the lake. Western meadowlarks probe the grassy slopes and mallards and kingfishers frolic at lake's edge.

Don't come expecting flower displays, for grasses and rock outcrops dominate here. This journey over the mysterious Orland Buttes and along Black Butte Lake is full of solitude, especially during winter and early spring. By late May, this exposed area gets miserably hot and full of stickers, and the views get hazy. Mountain bikers share this trail.

From I-5, take the main Orland exit (signed for Highway 32), and drive west on Newville Road. After 7.9 miles, turn left and follow

Orland Buttes and Black Butte Lake, late winter

the signs for Eagle Pass for the last mile. Park in the large lot at the paved road's end.

Pick up the faint path that promptly leads to a small, silver gate and continues straight up the highest rim in sight. Upon reaching the valley oak that is one-third wider than it is tall, wander over to a large boulder outcrop surrounded by a cluster of redbud shrubs (a sea of magenta flowers on bare stems in early April). The prime views here are of Bully Choop Mountain in the Klamath Mountains, one of the Orland Buttes, and a scenic strip of Black Butte Lake.

A panorama unfolds atop the rim 100 yards farther, where the Cascade Range caps the fertile Upper Sacramento Valley to the east. The Sutter Buttes punctuate the skyline to the south while the Yolla Bolly Mountains, usually snowcapped into April, dominate to the northwest. Note that the lightly wooded, smooth-sloped foothills march up to the steep and darker slopes of the Coast Ranges to the west. Countless clusters of large, lichen-coated basalt boulders accentuate the views. Poison oak, pipevine, coffeeberry, and squat interior live oaks complement the landscape.

Descend the grassy slope, angling toward an old dirt ranch road at lakeside, and note the trail on the left that can be used as a return route. Admire metallic gray Black Butte Lake, where grasses extend flush to the shore during high lake levels. Fishing for crappie and catfish here is usually good. At 1.5 miles, reach a colony of randomly scattered valley oaks along the shoreline, where another basalt butte rim features 100-foot-tall cliffs nearby to the east.

The level lakeside stroll continues another 1.5 miles to Orland Buttes Campground. On the return trip, vary your route by walking a trail that leads right, briefly climbing a grassy ridge. Black Butte Lake offers two other hikes that are shorter—Big Oak Trail at the southern end of the lake and Buckhorn Trail starting from Buckhorn Campground.

21 ❦ NORTH RIM TRAIL AND BIG CHICO CREEK

Distance: 8.4-mile loop
Difficulty: Easy to moderate
High point: 1200 feet
Elevation gain: 800 feet (high point is 1200 feet)
Maps: USGS Richardson Springs, Paradise
Nearest campground: Buckhorn Campground, phone (530) 865-4781
Information: City of Chico Parks Division, phone (530) 895-4962

This hike's constant vertical rock scenery looks more like a small-scale Grand Canyon than wild Northern California country. When the parade of statuesque blue oak trees leaf out in March and April, they can look like a city of faded blue flowers, especially when late afternoon sunlight backlights the branches.

The first and last miles of this hike in Bidwell Park are typically full of Chico area recreationists, including mountain bikers, fishermen, and folks on horses, and the countryside reminds a hiker of Chico's close proximity. The other 6 miles offer sheer remoteness, wild and rugged, featuring wondrous panoramas and an intimate stroll

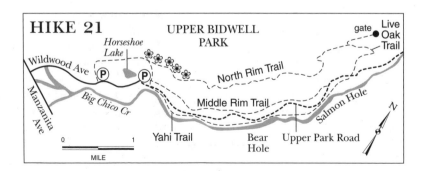

Looking east from North Rim Trail, late winter

close to restless and untamed Big Chico Creek. Huge, lichen-encrusted cliffs march in rows high above the creek, unraveling into the basalt-rimmed canyons. Numerous large flows of lava and mud from the Cascade Range deposited this rock several million years ago.

From Highway 99 in Chico, take the East Avenue exit. Head east on East Avenue (it eventually becomes Manzanita Avenue) for 2.8 miles, and turn left onto paved Wildwood Avenue. After 1.7 miles, turn into the second parking lot on the left at the gate.

To access the hike's start at the North Rim Trail, take one of three trails that promptly climb north from Horseshoe Lake. The goal is then to head off trail southeast along the ridge to perch upon the largest volcanic rock outcrop visible from the parking lot. The photogenic views here are mostly of Horseshoe Lake, Chico, and the Yolla Bolly Mountains to the west.

Climb gently to the ridge top to regain North Rim Trail and turn right. This wide-open ridgetop section is accentuated with occasional specimens of large and crazily twisted gray pines and squat blue oaks. Early spring presents a plethora of popcorn flower, lupine, fiddleneck, filaree, butter and eggs, and goldfields. Soon, the trail lingers on the ridge top's southern lip, revealing a multitude of dear scenes down on the open and U-shaped Big Chico Creek Canyon. The alplike Sutter Buttes form a miniature mountain range that accentuates the view to the south. Be sure to wander past the ceanothus shrubs (small white flowers in early spring) for lots of loving looks down into this oak- and pine-dotted canyon.

Spring flowering natives brodiaea and wild celery appear soon after the ridge narrows noticeably where drifts of poison oak shrubs and larger buckeyes are dwarfed next to oddly shaped boulders. At 4 miles, take the Live Oak Trail to the right. It is half the width of the dirt tread you've been on. Follow it as it switchbacks down the canyon, and toyon, manzanita, and interior live oak join the other tree and shrub species.

After 1 mile, meet the dirt Upper Park Road and continue downward to a lip offering a spectacular view down on raging Big Chico Creek, encased here in a steep and rocky gorge. Descend past a meadow flanked on the south side of Big Chico Creek by a vertical basalt cliff face. Then continue on the road and bear left to reach Salmon Hole at 5.7 miles. Popular Salmon Hole offers a swimming hole 25 yards wide by 25 yards long, a small and sandy beach, and the privacy of being tucked beneath steep basalt cliffs.

Nearby Yahi Trail, a scant path that traces the cliff's edge, offers great views down on a wild stretch of the creek and leads down to another swimming spot at 6.4 miles called Bear Hole. Big Chico Creek mellows from here, adorned by valley oaks, sycamores, white alders, cottonwoods, willows, bay laurels, and redbuds. Yahi Trail stays mostly level with the creek the rest of the way.

22 🌿 ROY ROGERS TRAIL TO LAKE OROVILLE

Distance: 5- to 6-mile loop
Difficulty: Easy to moderate
High point: 1100 feet
Elevation gain: 500 feet
Map: USGS Big Bend Mountain
Nearest campground: Bidwell Canyon Campground or Loafer
   Creek Campground, phone (530) 538-2200
Information: Lake Oroville State Recreation Area, phone (530)
   538-2200

The Oroville foothills are cheery green in early spring and golden brown in fall, and the Lake Oroville level fluctuations can be drastic but always scenic. This hike travels via gently sloping foothills dotted with pretty oaks to a cozy corner of Lake Oroville on two well-signed trails that are famous among horse riders in Butte County. Butte County features the widest variety of native shrubs and trees among

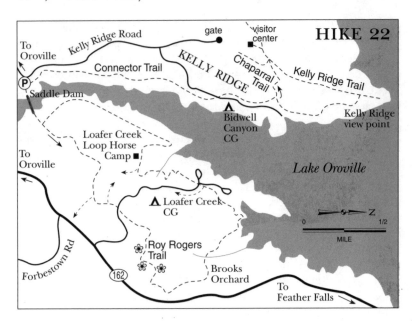

all California counties, and you'll find fifteen of the most common plants along the way.

Slender Loafer Creek Loop meanders and climbs gently along the foothill slopes, briefly through interior live oak woods followed by a mix of blue oak and live oak. Tall toyon and whiteleaf manzanita dominate the patchy understory, along with occasional coffeeberry, poison oak, and ceanothus. Buttercups and brodiaea blossom in the early spring.

In Oroville, drive to the intersection of Oroville Dam Boulevard and the Olive Highway (Highway 162). Travel the Olive Highway east for 5.4 miles, and turn north on paved Kelly Ridge Road. Just after the water treatment sign at 0.5 mile, park in the dirt lot just off the road.

As you begin this hike, there are a few things to consider. A bit of poison oak grows near some trail portions and two patches of star thistle border the trail. Also the occasional sound of cars on the Olive Highway can be heard on the first part of the trip. Start by walking to the other side of Saddle Dam, and then follow the Loafer Creek Loop in the direction indicated for Brooks Orchard. Continue straight at an unsigned trail junction at 0.8 mile featuring an inaugural view of Lake Oroville next to a stalwart ponderosa pine. In another 0.3 mile, reach a signed trail junction in a small clearing decorated with ceanothus and gargantuan gray pines. Continue straight.

The woods become dense along a gentle descent, passing two side trails, crossing a road, and eventually coming to Brooks Orchard at 2.4 miles, a clearing with hitching posts, picnic tables, and a water tank, all surrounded by healthy and scenic oaks and pines. You are now on Roy Rogers Trail, which soon crosses a stream and comes close to a skinny finger of Lake Oroville. Follow a dry streambed a bit farther along the trail to access the Bermuda-grass-covered shore. This wide-open, photogenic scene beckons to be explored for 1 or 2 miles. Admire the perfectly curved shoreline, the sapphire hue of Lake Oroville, the scattered Fremont cottonwood specimens, and the densely clothed and tapered hills beyond.

As the trail veers away from the lake, it soon skirts Loafer Creek Campground and passes between a pair of grand valley oaks at 3.4 miles. Cross the road and look west to spy the boat harbor. Look closely at a stream crossing for a brief, sheltered and shaded stretch where the foothill vegetation changes to black oaks, canyon live oaks, ponderosa pines, and buckeyes. Bear sharply right at the two signed trail junctions at 4 miles and climb briefly past large manzanita followed by glimpses of a long arm of Lake Oroville. Then skirt the restroom and tables at Horse Camp. The final mile continues along the open and grassy ridge (wildflowers in spring) with views of Kelly Ridge to the west and the grayish green, densely vegetated slope to the east, before descending to Saddle Dam.

Lake Oroville, autumn

23 ⚘ FREY CREEK AND FEATHER FALLS

Distance: 8.8-mile loop
Difficulty: Moderate
High point: 2400 feet
Elevation gain: 900 feet
Maps: USGS Forbestown, Brush Creek
Nearest campground: Loafer Creek Campground, phone (530) 538-2200
Information: LaPorte Ranger District, Plumas National Forest, phone (530) 675-2462

It's no secret—lots of folks gather to gawk at mighty Feather Falls in action. This 640-foot-long silver streak ranks sixth highest in the United States (not including Alaska), and fourth highest in California. Each step of the way is high quality; every highlight, and there are plenty, is meaningful. In addition to the spring wildflowers and countless views, Frey Creek rushes past you at several points, and it includes its own waterfall, modest compared to Feather Falls, but just as picturesque. Visit in the autumn for an incomparable display of fall color. Mountain bikers also use this trail.

From Highway 70 in Oroville, head east on Oroville Dam Boulevard and turn right after 1.7 miles onto the Olive Highway (Highway 162). After 6.8 miles, turn right onto paved Forbestown Road. Drive 6.2 miles, and then turn left onto paved Lumpkin Road. Travel a

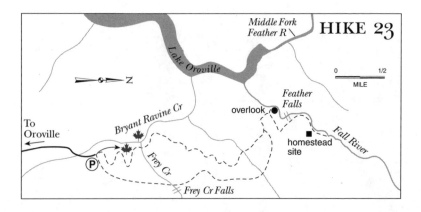

winding 11 miles, turn left onto the paved road signed for Feather Falls, and drive 1.6 miles to the large parking lot.

The wide and well-made footpath begins descending through a mixed hardwood and softwood forest. After going left at a signed trail junction (the trail on the right will be your return route should you choose to hike the loop trail), you reach a boulder patch shaded by a handsome, ancient live oak. Note the depressions in the rocks called mortars. Created over the last 2,000 years by the Maidu Indians, they were used for grinding acorns and nuts.

Within a 100 yards, look for a few of the rare California nutmeg conifers with their Douglas fir–like needles, but sharp to the touch. This shaded and tranquil mixed forest section displays fine specimens of California's most exquisite yellow pine belt native trees. The dogwoods, bigleaf maples, and black oaks are divinely yellow and orange in the fall. Incense cedar mingles with Douglas fir and the occasional ponderosa pine. Tan oaks and smooth-barked madrone continue to decorate the mostly steep stroll down to the scenic union of Bryant Ravine and Frey Creeks at 1.1 mile. A few pleasingly fragrant California bay laurel trees complement this setting next to a wooden bridge.

The trail now departs the moss-coated boulders nestled in cozy and modest Bryant Ravine Creek and follows a brief downhill stretch of surging Frey Creek, highlighted by continuous rapids and a few tiny waterfalls and cascades that bound into refreshing, clear pools. The steep canyon hosting Middle Fork Feather River appears from a vista point at 1.3 miles. The sheer cliff in the distance is Bald Rock Dome, revered by the Maidu Indians and still used as a North American Indian meditation site.

As the trail snakes down and away from the creek, it passes into an open forest woodland where occasional styrax, toyon, and snowberry bushes and interior live oak thrive above modest colonies of Indian pink, shooting star, yarrow, and bleeding heart flowers. Ivylike wild ginger adorns the more shaded seasonal stream crossings. Consider splashing some of the cool waters onto your face before the steady 1.3-mile climb to the ridge top.

Having completed the climb, pause at a ridgetop overlook next to orange bush monkeyflower and manzanita to ponder a spectacular strip of the roaring Fall River as it flows along a steep, wooded canyon and into an arm of Lake Oroville. But, ah, the best is yet to come. Walk for 5 minutes past moss-covered boulders and canyon live oaks to arrive at the wooden observation deck and be absolutely mesmerized

Feather Falls, spring

by free falling Feather Falls. The completely vertical crash of the falls creates an expansive, steamlike mist. There is no pool at the bottom, as is the case with most waterfalls. Instead, the frothy foam explodes off the rocky surface, and then careens over gigantic, slippery boulders.

A good side trail leads 0.25 mile to near the top of the falls and an old homestead site. A short but careful scramble to a flat rock offers an intimate feel for the falls, but photos of it are better from the observation deck.

If you choose to do the loop (recommended), retrace your steps down from the ridge top, but take the left trail junction instead of continuing to the canyon bottom. The return route along the loop is 1.2 miles longer, but with only a few mellow ups and downs. In the spring especially, you'll be rewarded with sightings of wild ginger, more of the other wildflowers, and beautiful lupines, while staying high along the canyonside. The manzanita grows taller (up to 20 feet high), the glances into the Frey Creek drainage are more frequent, and the encore presentation of Bald Rock Dome is more awesome. This trail eventually reaches a wooden bridge crossing, which shows off Frey Creek Falls.

LASSEN PEAK AREA
AND THE CASCADES

24 ⚘ CRYSTAL SPRINGS AND SPATTER CONE

Distance: 8 miles round trip; 3.2 miles round trip to Ja She Creek
Difficulty: Easy to moderate
High point: 3470 feet
Elevation gain: 400 feet
Maps: USGS Fall River Mills, Timbered Crater
Nearest campground: McArthur-Burney Falls Memorial State Park, phone (530) 335-2777
Information: McArthur-Burney Falls Memorial State Park, phone (530) 335-2777

You will need a boat to take advantage of this hike. Indeed, it takes a wonderful, mile-long canoe ride to venture into surreal looking, volcanic, view-filled, and waterbird-occupied Ahjumawi Lava Springs State Park. The boat portion of the trip follows huge Horr Pond westerly, revealing continuous views of these gray waters to the south and beyond to fertile grasslands and prominent volcanic peaks. Learn interesting human history from signboards at Crystal Springs, Ja She Creek, and an abandoned homestead beyond a large meadow. Later on this hike, visit basaltic rock hills and chaotic jumbles, enter a lava tube cave, and clamber along the rim of a spatter cone.

Consider bringing binoculars to study the variety of waterbirds that feed, glide, and cruise at Horr Pond and neighboring Big Lake, especially in late fall. Mating season is in full swing during early to midspring. Watch for white pelicans, Canada geese, blue herons, teals, ospreys, and mallards. Keep in mind that getting to the trailhead often requires a four-wheel drive if heavy winter rains have hit in the past 10 days or so. Also be warned that hunting season lasts from early October to mid-January.

From McArthur, just east of Fall River Mills on Highway 299, take Main Street north to a dirt road that swings right past a gate and a canal after 0.5 mile. Continue for 3 miles to the large dirt parking lot.

Cast away in your canoe or other watercraft and head northwest, directly toward Mount Shasta, until you spy the campground toward the right near the shore. Join the Lava Springs Trail here and follow this wide dirt path west beneath white oaks, black oaks, and western junipers. Your gaze will automatically steer southward, as you appreciate the waterbirds frolicking and feeding in front of Prospect, West Prospect, and Lassen Peaks, Thousand Lakes summits, and Burney Mountain.

Continue straight past the first trail junction at 0.5 mile, and at 0.7 mile note a lava rock foundation beneath some tall ponderosa pines. Various herbs including horehound, mullein, stinging nettle, plantain, and mugwort and occasional fruit trees indicate signs of past homesteading along the route. Native shrubs nestled among the lava boulders scattered at trailside and growing out of various conic depressions include redbud, ceanothus, sagebrush, and bitterbrush.

At 1.1 miles, Crystal Springs originates from the side of the trail and is studded with large lava rocks assembled like stepping stones. For thousands of years (and sometimes even now), the Ahjumawi Indians used these rocks as fish traps for catching *Lat he* (Sacramento sucker fish). The Ahjumawi blocked the opening of the trap, and then caught fish with spears, nets, and bare hands. This rare rock weir is promptly followed by an old, abandoned homestead and a campsite in a grassy clearing.

Reach a bridge and crystal clear Ja She Creek at 1.6 miles, featuring a wide outlet resembling a shallow lake. The dark boulder bottom and the oak- and willow-lined shore create a unique scenic setting. The source of the pure waters of Ja She Creek (meaning where the

Horr Pond near Crystal Springs, autumn

little tules grow) is believed to be 50 miles south at Tule Lake. The final mile of this trail veers away from Horr Pond and traipses through a large meadow where Mount Shasta soon appears above assorted cattails, willows, and conifers. The path peters out at a large, old, abandoned homestead with a big barn—you might see a barn owl fly out.

Retrace your steps, but turn left on Lava Springs Trail at 4.7 miles, 0.5 mile before you reach your boat. The trail heads north initially in a sparse forest of oak and juniper. You soon enter the surreal realm of lava land, where the bare black basalt forms a solemn landscape. Stay left at the fork at 5.2 miles to follow Spatter Cone Loop Trail. Note a cluster of large mountain mahoganies thriving at trailside. A half mile farther, note a sign and then reach a small cave formed by a remnant of a lava tube that was created thousands of years ago. Explore this cool, 30-foot-deep and 15-foot-wide cave, and then exit, climbing moderately. You'll soon reach the first full view of Mount Shasta. At 6.1 miles, climb to the rim of the spatter cone, which measures 20 feet deep and 100 feet across. Retrace your steps or continue on the loop trail. If you have time, there are also other trails to explore.

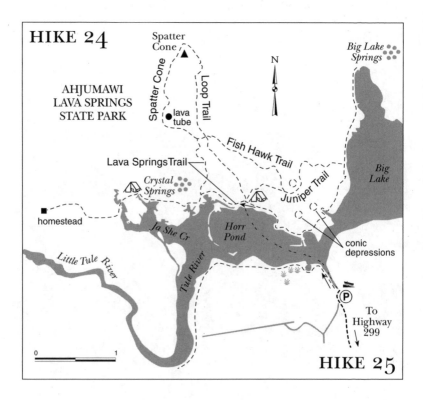

25 🌿 HORR POND TO TULE RIVER

Distance: 5.2 miles round trip
Difficulty: Easy
High Point: 3300 feet
Elevation gain: 50 feet
Map: USGS Fall River Mills
Nearest campground: McArthur-Burney Falls Memorial State Park,
    phone (530) 335-2777
Information: McArthur-Burney Falls Memorial State Park, phone
    (530) 335-2777

See Hike 25 map on p. 88.

This level levee walk is like being at a miniature Tule Lake, but the views are better. Expect to see a plethora of waterbirds—you won't be disappointed. There are times in autumn when Horr Pond, the neighboring swamp, and the Tule River are teeming with a vast array of winged creatures that seem right out of an Audubon book. Consider bringing binoculars anytime in the off-season to admire elegant Canada geese, swooping blue herons, soaring teals, gliding ospreys, cruising mallards, patrolling red-tailed hawks, long-beaked pelicans, and assorted others. Prepare to witness the sudden rise of a tremendous flock of waterfowl or to hear a rousing chorus of high-pitched cries.

Dome-shaped volcanoes—large and small, near and far—are in constant view to the west and south. Most are often snowcapped from winter into early spring, adding a touch of cool mountain air to the mostly flat landscape of water and grasslands along this hike. Keep in mind that getting to the trailhead often requires a four-wheel drive if heavy winter rains have hit in the past 10 days or so. Also be warned that hunting season lasts from early October to mid-January. There are far fewer folks midweek during these months.

Drive to McArthur, just east of Fall River Mills on Highway 299. Take Main Street north to a dirt road that swings right past a gate and a canal after 0.5 mile. Continue for 3 miles to the large dirt parking lot.

Begin on the wide cinder trail heading northwest, which switches to chalky white in 1 mile. Scan for bird activity over spacious, blue gray Horr Pond (a continuance of Big Lake) on the right and a small pond at 0.5 mile on the left. A large swamp with abundant cattails soon shows up on the left, where smaller birds scurry across mudflats. Major bird fanciers pick spots between Horr Pond and this large swamp

Tule River, autumn

to zoom in on sandhill cranes, white pelicans, cackling geese, northern shovelers, and northern pintails.

Mount Shasta glistens across Horr Pond in the distance. Directly to the west, nearby Soldier, Saddle, and Haney Mountains (from north to south) occasionally get snow. A stretch of massive volcanoes line the southern skies from Burney Mountain to Crater Peak (Thousand Lakes area) and onward to Lassen Peak.

The flat trail swerves southward at 1.4 miles, following the gently curving Tule River past pastoral settings of barns and farm fields, indicators of the Fall River Valley's fertility. Only an occasional willow lines the grassy riverbanks. Reach a narrow stretch of the Tule River at 2.6 miles and note the Little Tule River across the banks joining the flow. If more hiking is desired, retrace your steps to the trailhead and continue northeast on another wide cinder trail. It explores the shores of Big Lake, which owes its existence to the porous lava rock that makes up much of the Modoc Plateau. Water from the Tule Lake region of northeastern California travels underground 50 miles through this porous rock to emerge here.

26 ⚘ BURNEY FALLS AND LAKE BRITTON

Distance: 5-mile figure-eight loop
Difficulty: Easy to moderate
High point: 3000 feet
Elevation gain: 400 feet
Map: USGS Burney Falls
Nearest campground: McArthur-Burney Falls Memorial State Park,
   phone (530) 335-2777
Information: McArthur-Burney Falls Memorial State Park, phone
   (530) 335-2777

Mighty Burney Falls are twin cascades that vertically plunge 129 feet into a deep and large sapphire pool. Creamy streams of water flow from the sides of the falls over moss and rock, supplementing breathtaking falls that are known worldwide. A vast underground reservoir feeds Burney Creek a daily supply of several million gallons of crystal, cold water. This hike takes you to three special vantage points for photographing these spring-fed falls.

You'll follow trails that trace the course of swift and powerful Burney Creek on both sides, passing fishermen, and traipse in deep forest to Lake Britton, which features a rare combination of fish for

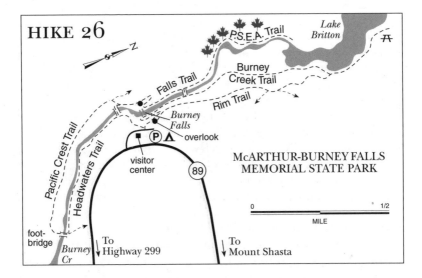

a mountain lake, including crappie, trout, bass, and bluegill. In the autumn, cherish the brilliant colors of the dogwoods, vine maples, and black oaks. In winter, when you're apt to have the whole place to yourself on a weekday, slippery ice sometimes forms in shady spots along the trail.

From the junction of Highways 299 and 89, 54 miles east of I-5, drive north on Highway 89 for 6 miles. Turn left and follow the signs for McArthur-Burney Falls Memorial State Park.

Find the trail near the visitor center and go right.

The first view of massive and wide Burney Falls comes right away via the falls overlook. Watch for black swifts darting amazingly near the surging cascades. An asphalt

Burney Falls, autumn

path snakes down to the bottom of the falls, where you can sniff deeply as the residual spray caresses and cools your face.

Stroll along this main path as it leaves the falls behind, passing by flowering currant (white flowers in spring) and huge chunks of moss-covered basalt talus that fell and piled up from the cliff rim above. At 0.4 mile reach a bridge and a trail junction. Continue straight and follow Burney Creek Trail in a forest of ponderosa pine, Douglas fir, incense cedar, Oregon white oak, and black oak. Stay left at 0.9 mile where the Rim Trail to the right climbs in forest back to the campground and trailhead (an option for shortening the hike). Continue another 0.3 mile to a swimming beach at Lake Britton, a shimmering lake set in a gorge. Note the lake water is much warmer than chilly Burney Creek.

Retrace your steps to the footbridge, cross it and go right on the P.S.E.A. Trail, which stays intimately close to Burney Creek and features several creekside spots ideal for watching the water flow. White alder, vine maple, and dogwood abound all the way to the trail's end at a gate (2.5 miles), with sections of chalky diatomaceous earth at trailside.

Return to the footbridge, but instead of crossing it, follow the Falls Trail upward past thimbleberry, vine maples, dogwoods, and bear clover to another view across the slope to Burney Falls. Upon reaching a trail fork, turn right and then left to get on the Pacific Crest Trail (3.4 miles), which you follow 0.7 mile to a bridge across Burney Creek. Note that little water flows here; most enters from springs downstream. Turn left onto the Headwaters Trail, which heads past greenleaf manzanita and deer brush (white flowers in spring) for a half mile along the banks and near the top of the falls. Go left to the middle of the bridge, where you can see the surging rapids preparing to plunge off the precipice.

27 🍃 CRYSTAL AND BAUM LAKES

Distance: 5 miles round trip
Difficulty: Easy
High point: 3000 feet
Elevation gain: 100 feet
Map: USGS Cassel
Nearest campground: Cassel Campground, phone 1-800-743-5000
Information: Pacific Gas and Electric, P.O. Box 277444, Sacramento, CA 95826

The placid waters of Crystal and Baum Lakes clearly reflect the ominous visages of Burney Mountain to the west and Mount Shasta to the north. The lakes offer a tranquil place where osprey, hawks, and

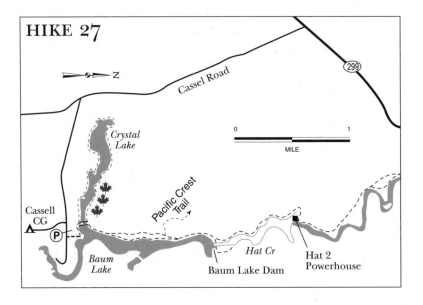

HIKE 27

Crystal Lake, autumn

migratory ducks and geese soar aloft. Fishermen like it, too. Take a twilight trip and hope for an award-winning sunset, quite common in spring and fall when cumulus and cirrus clouds hover on the horizon. The trail network traces the lakes' shorelines, showing off hatchery-released rainbow and brook trout. The level trail can muddy your boots during and after rain or snow in winter and early spring. You don't need the trail when it's covered with snow.

From the intersection of Highways 299 and 89, 54 miles east of I-5, drive Highway 299 east for 2 miles and turn south onto paved Cassel Road. Go 2 more miles and turn left at the sign for Crystal Lake Fish Hatchery. Drive another mile and then turn left into the paved parking lot.

Traipse over to the dam that separates the two lakes. Cross the dam to the north side and then take the trail left to skirt the shore of photogenic Crystal Lake. For the first mile or so, western juniper, sagebrush, squawbush, and ceanothus accompany you, along with Oregon white oak and black oak, which display attractive shades of orange and rust in midautumn. The next mile along the south side of the lake returns you to your starting point as it passes through an open ponderosa pine forest where clear views of Mount Shasta are frequent. Look for white pelicans patrolling the gray waters of Crystal Lake.

Your other choice from the north side of the dam is the 1.5-mile path along Baum Lake's west shore, which includes a portion of the Pacific Crest Trail. Follow the obvious narrow trail north, and note ponderosa pines growing close to the water's edge while deciduous oaks dominate the slopes on the left.

The way soon splits. The upper trail travels midslope, crosses a fence, and then reaches another fork. The Pacific Crest Trail heads left and uphill from this midslope trail, but you stay right and soon reach the lower trail, which always runs along the lakeshore.

Continue along the leaf-littered path past lava rock talus, negotiate a brush area along a small creek, and then reach Baum Lake Dam. For more hiking, continue north along the canal to soon reach Hat 2 Powerhouse, cross the dam and follow the trail some 400 yards down to Hat Creek's banks.

28 🌿 HAT CREEK TRAIL

Distance: 8.6 miles round trip
Difficulty: Easy
High point: 4300 feet
Elevation gain: 400 feet
Map: USGS Old Station
Nearest campground: Cave Campground, phone (530) 336-5521
Information: Hat Creek Ranger District, Lassen National Forest,
    phone (530) 336-5521

Hat Creek's amazing journey into the Pit River begins as snowmelt high on the north-facing flank of Lassen Peak. The creek's crystal clear waters beautify Paradise Meadows, widen into a marsh that was once Hat Lake, and finally become the swift force that you follow along this hike. Come exploring late in the year and the numerous cascades and tiny waterfalls are tame compared to spring's robust burst. This hike done in early winter reveals a pleasant and mild Hat Creek, and a hiker's thoughts will tend toward carefree daydreams. When there's enough snow, try cross-country skis or snowshoes. In late spring, this part of the creek is a constant, loud crash that stirs the senses—toss in a stick and watch it vanish instantly in the surge.

From the junction of Highways 44 and 89 near Old Station, turn north onto Highway 89 and drive 0.3 mile. Turn left into Cave Campground, go 30 yards, and park in the small lot on the left. Cross the wooden bridge at Hat Creek and pick up the trail on the right. The trail reaches a concrete bridge and a gorge of rapidly rushing water in 0.5 mile, where a cluster of tall ponderosa pines thrives. Hemmed into a narrow slot by solid lava rock, this series of cascades and mini-waterfalls plunge, race, and crash loudly into a fast flowing, wider channel. Other less spectacular gorges and rapids promptly ensue as the sandy and mostly flat trail follows its exciting downward journey. The path rarely wanders farther than a few yards from Hat Creek.

Look for a gorgeous grove of white-trunked aspen trees at 1 mile.

Hat Creek, late spring

It's odd to see so many towering ponderosa pines and incense cedars, two species that basically detest wet feet, interspersed with aspens and other riparian trees such as alders and willows. Just a few yards beyond the banks, there's an uninterrupted maze of chaparral shrubs such as greenleaf manzanita, antelope bitterbrush, mountain mahogany, and rabbit goldenweed, dotted with western junipers and California sage.

The shrubs drastically outnumber the trees and partially shield the continuous views. Sugarloaf Peak to the west is the most prominent mountain at first. The glimpses of Lassen Peak are more obvious on the return trip. The west facing visage of Hat Creek Rim is a constant companion. Views of Freaner Peak and Burney Mountain farther northwest become more frequent after reaching a second but smaller aspen grove at 1.8 miles, followed by a rock-encased cascade 0.2 mile farther.

After passing another little waterfall at 2.2 miles, the trail briefly enters a forest strip of conifers as well as the occasional white fir and sugar pine, with a snowberry-dominated ground cover. A steady cascade splashes over narrow and rocky banks for 0.25 mile, decreasing only after culminating in another small waterfall at 2.7 miles.

At 3.1 miles, the first sighting of Magee and Crater Peaks to the west are featured from a vantage point near some aspens and a huge, multiple-trunked alder tree. Some thimbleberry graces the trailside as you enter another forest strip that promptly leads to a wooden bridge and Rocky Campground at 3.8 miles. Adding visual variety, the trail then dissects some basalt talus and rises gently so you can look down into the canyon to admire Hat Creek until you reach Bridge Camp at 4.3 miles.

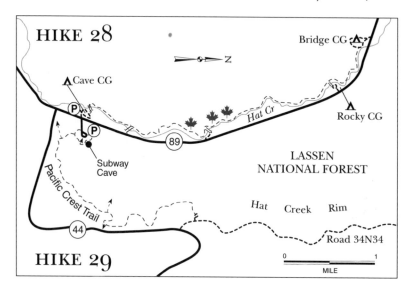

29 ❧ HAT CREEK RIM AND SUBWAY CAVE

Distance: 7 miles round trip
Difficulty: Moderate
High point: 4900 feet
Elevation gain: 600 feet
Map: USGS Old Station
Nearest campground: Cave Campground, phone (530) 336-5521
Information: Hat Creek Ranger District, Lassen National Forest,
    phone (530) 336-5521

It's an interesting privilege to wander in this high desert transition zone, where open forest interacts with dry, flat highlands blanketed with tiny-leafed, tough shrubs. As you approach and then climb Hat Creek Rim, you experience this treat as well as views of a young cinder cone volcano (Sugarloaf Mountain), a plug dome volcano (Lassen Peak), and a shield dome volcano (West Prospect Peak). The rim is cooler in fall and spring months, when there are also fewer people. Sometimes in winter, after a cold snow, hikers don snowshoes or cross-country skis. There is no water available along the trail, so fill up at the faucet in the parking lot.

Enjoy the striking contrast as you trade the sunglasses needed in Hat Creek Rim's open territory for the flashlight required to shed light into pitch-black Subway Cave. Sure, you can explore this long rock channel to start, but consider saving it as a final reward. Note the useful information provided by the interpretive signs scattered throughout the cave.

From the junction of Highways 44 and 89 near Old Station, turn north onto Highway 89 and drive 0.3 mile. Turn right onto the paved Subway Cave access road (across from Cave Campground), drive 200 yards, and park in the large paved lot.

Soon after the trail starts, go left at the junction with the Rattlesnake Collapse section of the Subway Cave entry, and then follow the wide path 300 yards. Bear left onto the unsigned Pacific Crest Trail at 0.5 mile, next to a dual-trunked Jeffrey pine tree. This long and flat stretch of wide trail is laden with cinders that have disintegrated into a sandy substance in some places. Listen for the amusing crunch of your footsteps while staring at West Prospect Peak to the right and Sugarloaf Peak to the left. You're on the westernmost range of California's high desert, typified by abundant antelope bitterbrush and occasional rabbit goldenweed at trailside. Many of the pine trees are somewhat stunted here, especially next to greenleaf manzanita and fragrant desert sage.

The trail is briefly interrupted by a downed conifer at 1.7 miles, next to a trio of attractive conifers—a splendid white fir dwarfed by a more ancient western juniper and a taller ponderosa pine. The rugged slopes of Hat Creek Rim take center stage here. This 900-foot-high, 14-mile-long escarpment was formed when the earth ripped along a fault and was thrust up on one side.

Bear right at a major but unsigned trail junction 2 miles into the hike. Twelve-foot-tall mountain mahogany shrubs dominate, and there is a magnificent, tall sugar pine 30 yards to the right (look for the foot-long cones). At 2.4 miles, room-sized lava slabs appear on each side of the trail, just past a slide of dark basaltic rocks. Pass another trail junction on the right and continue on the main trail. Highway 44 is quite close and just above here, but the traffic sounds are so faint that it's hardly noticeable. The way now climbs in earnest, but thankfully swerves out of sight and sound of the highway. Take periodic breathers and gaze behind you for occasionally unobstructed views of Lassen Peak and Chaos Crags.

Upon reaching the lower level of Hat Creek Rim at 3 miles, the climbing is virtually complete. The highly mineralized and porous

Lassen Peak from Hat Creek Rim, late spring

soil is comfortably soft here. By wandering off the beaten path at opportune intervals, a hiker can gain unique and appealing views of Mount Shasta, Burney Valley, Freaner Peak, and the Hat Creek Valley, all to the northwest.

Return to Subway Cave, take out your flashlight, and climb down the cement steps into the 1300-foot-long lava tube. Note the shallow puddles (from ceiling leaks) and the embedded pumice on the rocky floor. Wander into halls, chambers, tunnels, and cul-de-sacs in search of lavacicles hanging from the ceiling, burst lava bubbles, and partial collapses.

The cave formed some 30,000 years ago when lava began spewing from deep cracks in the earth. Rivers of molten, red-hot rock then crawled northward, covering the floor of Hat Creek Valley. While the top crust cooled and hardened, the red-hot lava rivers, insulated by the newly formed rock above, continued to flow. Eventually the lava drained, leaving tubelike caves, such as Subway Cave, the largest accessible tube in the flow. The Atsugewi Indians discovered the cave long ago and believed it to be inhabited by an evil, apelike creature. This may be a good anecdote to relate to your fellow hikers deep within the cave.

30 SUSAN RIVER

Distance: 13 miles round trip
Difficulty: Easy
High point: 4660 feet
Elevation gain: 500 feet
Maps: USGS Susanville, Roop Mountain
Nearest campground: Merrill Campground, phone (530) 257-2151
Information: Eagle Lake Resource Area, Bureau of Land Management, phone (530) 257-0456

The Bizz Johnson Trail follows an abandoned railroad line, offering a comfortable, up close and personal way to explore a scenic stretch of the Susan River. Thanks to the idea of legendary outdoorsman John Reginato and the work of the Bureau of Land Management, the former Lassen and Fernley railroad lines were converted into a 30-mile-long trail. This hike covers the trail's eastern portion, reaching Devils Corral just off Highway 36, 7 miles west of Susanville. To shorten this hike by half, arrange for a car to meet you at Devils Corral. Visit in autumn to enjoy splashes of riverside color, or wait for a good snowfall and follow the example of students from nearby Lassen College—don cross-country skis and glide along this wide, flat trail.

In Susanville, turn south on Weatherlow Street, which soon becomes Richmond Road. After 0.5 mile, park across from the historic Susanville Railroad Depot.

Consider the first mile of this dirt trail a warm-up, passing behind a couple of neighborhoods before crossing a rustic metal bridge above a lovely swimming spot in a lazy part of the Susan River. Vertical, jagged cliffs of sheer rock are like a shrine towering over the scene. This part

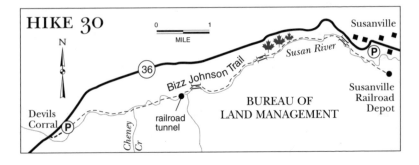

of the trail, like most of the trip, reveals a stark contrast between dry slopes and moist banks. Bitterbrush and sagebrush eke out existences between lichen-coated lava rocks, while willows and magnificently mature black cottonwoods clog the riverbanks. Black oak, western juniper, and elderberry are interspersed throughout the scene.

Cross the small, oil-stained wooden bridge at 1.5 miles, overlooking gravel-bar islands in the river. A forest of ponderosa pine decorates the far shore (now to your left), while occasional and shorter ponderosa pines join scattered black oaks on the mostly barren slope to the right. There may be a few frolicking local residents here, fishing in the spring or inner-tubing in the summer.

Bridge over Susan River

At 2.1 miles, the mostly exposed trail reaches a well-placed bench and a couple of spur trails leading to the almost-trailside creek. People are fewer from here on out as the hike reaches its prime—pristine wild country that gets whisper-quiet at times, save for the chirping of the birds or the passage of modest rapids. Perhaps the best and deepest swimming hole on this hike appears below a wood and concrete bridge at 2.8 miles. Note the wonderfully sloped and rugged canyonsides at the next bridge 150 yards farther. View nature's ideal mix of ponderosa pines above a black cottonwood grove, with random basalt boulder piles and a mosaic of chaparral shrubs. In winter and spring, look for the gorgeous seasonal stream 200 yards farther that cascades down the gentle north slope next to a dramatic basalt outcrop. A conifer-clad peak stands guard over an unnamed stream that flows into the river. At 3.8 miles there is a nice campsite on the far shore. Conifers begin shading creek sections, contrasting nicely with bright green willows and the shimmering, heart-shaped cottonwood leaves.

For the first time on the hike, the trail rises well above the river, which is interrupted on its course by closet-sized boulders. Cross another wooden bridge at 4.8 miles next to a marshy strip of the river. Then spend some hang time in an old railroad tunnel, which is naturally cool year-round. Builders had the dangerous task of blasting through pure rock to carve out this 150-yard-long tunnel, built in 1914. Trains once passed through its dark and echo-filled length to service the timber industry.

Once through the tunnel, peer behind you to admire the conglomerate of rocks forming a cliff and encasing the passageway. The next 1.5 or so miles to Devils Corral feature more of these highlights, including several swimming holes, more jumbles of lava rock, and a slender but long meadow strip of tall grasses.

31 ⚘ CINDER CONE

Distance: 5 miles round trip
Difficulty: Moderate
High point: 6900 feet
Elevation gain: 800 feet
Maps: USGS Prospect Peak, Mount Harkness
Nearest campground: Butte Lake Campground, phone (530) 336-5521
Information: Lassen Volcanic National Park, phone (530) 595-4444

The large lakes, acres of rock piles, and miniature hills that surround Cinder Cone make for a setting so surreal it's like visiting an alien world. Walk through this otherworldly setting and then look down on it from atop nearly symmetrical Cinder Cone, the centerpiece of this classic volcanic wonderland. This route can easily be extended into

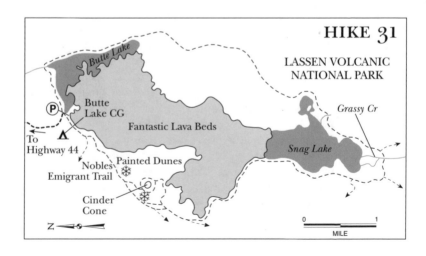

Painted Dunes from Cinder Cone, autumn

an awesome 14-mile day hike or backpack loop by wandering through the lodgepole pine, Jeffrey pine, and fir forest to shallow Snag Lake, then around the aspen-dotted eastern shore of deep blue Butte Lake. Water is available from campground faucets, but they are turned off during winter months so you're better off bringing water from home. If there's considerable snow, frequently the case from December into March, it's best to ski or snowshoe just to Cinder Cone. Heavy snow may also force you to park on the side of the road 1 or 2 miles short of the trailhead. Call ahead to check conditions.

From the junction of Highways 89 and 44 near Manzanita Lake, 49 miles east of I-5, take Highway 44 for 12 miles. Turn south on a gravel and cinder road signed for Butte Lake. Continue to the road's end 6.7 miles farther and park near Butte Lake's north shore.

To start, pick up the pamphlet that corresponds to numbered posts along the historic Nobles Emigrant Trail, which was used in the mid-1800s by thousands of pioneers. This loose cinder path wanders in an open conifer forest bordered by the tremendous piles of gray black basalt that form the Fantastic Lava Beds. Glassy fragments of quartz crystals helped shape these boulder hills, as lava from several Cinder Cone eruptions cooled.

Ancient Jeffrey and ponderosa pines tower over the adjacent flat forest floor here, with initial views of Lassen Peak and neighboring

Crescent Crater appearing at 0.4 mile. Look for the huge, photogenic white stump snag on the trail's right side (kids like to climb it) just before reaching the trail fork at Cinder Cone's base at 0.8 mile. Take the left fork to Cinder Cone and prepare for a climb. The steep, 700-foot ascent up Cinder Cone is made even more challenging because each footstep sinks and slips into porous cinders. Establish a patient trudge, and pause often to admire tree-covered Prospect Peak to the north and Lassen Peak to the west.

From atop Cinder Cone, three trails beckon. The 0.6-mile-long rim trail offers breathtaking views of Butte and Snag Lakes, separated by the Fantastic Lava Beds and the orange and gray ash piles called Painted Dunes. A shorter trail allows you to look down into the cavernous reverse cone in the center of Cinder Cone. Just beyond the northwest outer edge of the cone's rim, a handful of partially wind-protected mountain mahogany shrubs eke out an existence in the well-drained but nutrient-lean developing soil. This explains why the leaves are more yellow than green. A scattering of stunted lodgepole pines and a few even smaller Jeffrey pines stand out in an otherwise stark landscape of smooth and symmetrical rust- and gray-colored slopes. The third trail plunges some 100 feet down into the bottom of the charcoal-colored pit, which is studded with pumice and larger basalt rocks.

The main trail loops down to Cinder Cone's southern base. The trail then encircles the cone (use caution) in a delightfully alien-planet-like setting. Colored swirls of the Painted Dunes mingle with moonlike boulders of the Fantastic Lava Beds; odd-looking big rocks are strewn about with an occasional child-sized conifer punctuating the gray and brown landscape.

32 ⚬ MANZANITA CREEK

Distance: 6.8 miles round trip
Difficulty: Moderate
High point: 6900 feet
Elevation gain: 1100 feet
Maps: USGS Manzanita Lake, Lassen Peak
Nearest campground: Cave Campground, phone (530) 257-2151
Information: Lassen Volcanic National Park, phone (530) 595-4444

Being near the source of a high mountain creek is always scenic and exhilarating. Take this hike to the limit, even just beyond, and you're apt to agree. Along the way, you'll get head-on views of inhospitable

Chaos Crags from Manzanita Creek Trail, late spring

Chaos Crags, a volcano formed over a millenium ago when viscous lava welled up for more than 500 yards. You'll also explore a 1.5-mile-long stretch of Manzanita Creek, traipse through high meadows, and marvel at the mountain views.

Autumn allows the most solitude, and wildflowers persist despite drying meadows. Visit in winter or early spring for delightful and invigorating cross-country skiing or snowshoeing along the Manzanita Creek Trail. Skiing between regal firs laced with new snow is divine, and to zoom more than 4 miles downhill, virtually nonstop, is a maximum thrill.

From Redding, take Highway 44 east 48 miles and turn right into signed Lassen Volcanic National Park. Follow the paved road and signs for Manzanita Lake Campground (drive about 1 mile). There is a large year-round parking lot near the visitor center; add 2 miles to your trip if snow forces you to park here. Otherwise, continue as far as you can toward the campground and park in designated areas.

Before getting on the signed Manzanita Creek Trail, wander into the open field for unimpeded views of twin-peaked Chaos Crags. This large, flat field is a bizarre mosaic of juvenile Jeffrey pines, greenleaf manzanita, scattered tufts of native perennial grasses, and ghostly limbs of deceased manzanita.

It's best to establish a slow but deliberate pace as you climb consistently but moderately in an open Jeffrey pine and white fir forest. Backdoor views of Chaos Crags, Lassen Peak, and Eagle Peak kick in along a flat stretch of trail at 1.2 miles. These partially shielded glimpses soon disappear temporarily, but enjoy the whisperlike silence as you continue past evergreen sheets of pinemat manzanita and occasional bush chinquapin. Reach a medium-sized dry meadow at 1.6 miles, where the previously mentioned peaks reappear, flanking Crescent Crater and appearing closer at hand than they actually are. Western white pines join the understory as you stroll this meadow laden with lupine and fragrant coyote mint. Nature's ideal mix of white rapids and crystal clear water greet you at a bridge crossing at 1.9 miles. The refreshing murmur of swift and narrow Manzanita Creek sets a rhythm for the rest of the way. Loomis Peak, steep and imposing to the southwest, appears at 2.4 miles next to an expansive alder thicket. The trail, composed of disintegrating pumice cinders, now stays mostly flat past meadow strips loaded with corn lilies and bordered by lichen-covered red firs.

The trail narrows and eventually peters out where Manzanita Creek pours suddenly down a steep slope near the doorstep of colorful Loomis Peak. From this moist meadow, a backpacker has several crosscountry opportunities, including the circumnavigation of Lassen Peak and the exploration of nearby Vulcan's Castle and Crescent Cliff. If nothing else, leave the trail here and check out the most gorgeous stretch of Manzanita Creek, featuring miniwaterfalls, curving cascades, and bubbly whirlpools. Soothe your tired and sweaty feet with a barefoot soak in a bubbly part of the frigid creek (bet you can't keep 'em in longer than 30 seconds).

On the return trip, note the stark contrasts in form and texture between the Thousand Lakes mountain cluster to the north and nearby Loomis Peak.

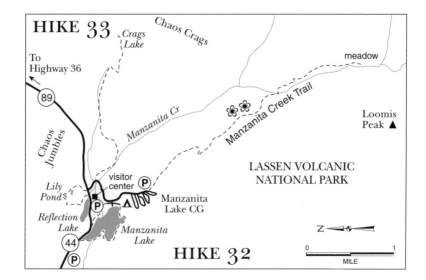

33 ❦ REFLECTION AND MANZANITA LAKES

Distance: 3.8 miles round trip
Difficulty: Easy
High point: 5900 feet
Elevation gain: 200 feet
Map: USGS Manzanita Lake
Nearest campground: Cave Campground, phone (530) 257-2151
Information: Lassen Volcanic National Park, phone (530) 595-4444

See Hike 33 map on p. 106.

Paradise is watching ducks glide across a high mountain lake, with a trio of volcanoes reflected perfectly in the clear, calm water. Hiking the shorelines of Reflection and Manzanita Lakes is like walking through an outdoor impressionist masterpiece. In late spring and early summer, lilies on aptly named Lily Pond boast magnificent chartreuse flowers. In winter and early spring, some or all of the lakes are iced over with a crown of snow, while bright blue Steller's jays squawk and thrash amid the willows and conifers along the shores. Skiers and snowshoers explore Manzanita Lake's shoreline on nice winter weekends, especially after snowfall. This paradise may belong only to you during autumn, when tourists suddenly vanish.

From Redding, take Highway 44 east for 48 miles and turn right into signed Lassen Volcanic National Park. Drive the paved road about 0.5 mile and park in the gravel lot at the visitor center. The signed trailhead is across the road near Reflection Lake.

Start the hike by following the 0.7-mile interpretive loop around Lily Pond through a mixed forest that reveals an impressive nine different kinds of native conifers. Informative leaflets are at the trailhead.

After finishing Lily Pond Trail, retrace your steps along the shore of Reflection Lake to post number 9 (beneath a graceful ponderosa pine giant). Then veer left on the slender trail that traces the shoreline. From a rush-lined beach strip on the northeastern shore of Reflection Lake, admire the view of Chaos Crags and Lassen Peak. This is an ideal perch for watching a full moon rise above these peaks to shimmer over the lake.

To access the Manzanita Lake Trail, follow the Reflection Lake Trail to the western shore, cross the park road and head south (left) on the new trail as it curves around Manzanita Lake. Note the numerous large pine logs that have fallen along this eastern shore—it will take

some 50 years for them to rot into a ground cover of wood chips. The trail then temporarily veers away from the lake next to a large grove of willows. Manzanita Creek widens along a sandy beach (nice place to wade and sunbathe) before easing into a shallow part of Manzanita Lake. Note the gargantuan ponderosa pine next to a pair of tables and an equally tall conifer snag followed by a section of sedge grasses.

Pass the launch site for nonmotorized boats and follow the trail as it hugs the shoreline for the lake's final mile. You'll frequently duck under white fir and Jeffrey pine and pass close to tiny saturated islands clogged with willow shrubs. After crossing a seasonal stream 0.8 mile along Manzanita Lake Trail, stay close to the southwestern shore. The lake is shallow here—excellent for dipping—and thickets of greenleaf manzanita are interspersed with rushes at water's edge. A colorful grove of black cottonwoods shimmer in the breeze along the shore just as views of Eagle Peak, Lassen Peak, and Chaos Crags appear.

Sensational, photogenic scenes of these peaks continue, and soon Loomis Peak joins the others on the right. These views disappear for 0.25 mile, but return triumphantly soon after crossing the lake's outlet stream (look for icicles after a clear night in winter). Take in a final splendid view of the aforementioned peaks near a rustic stone A-frame close to the park road. Although the trail continues around the lake, the section near the park road is mediocre compared to what you've just seen. It's best to retrace your steps from the A-frame and revisit the splendor of Manzanita Lake in reverse.

34 LOWER DEER CREEK FALLS

Distance: 4.6 miles round trip; 3.2 miles round trip to Lower Deer Creek Falls
Difficulty: Easy to moderate
High point: 3200 feet
Elevation gain: 600 feet
Map: USGS Onion Butte
Nearest campground: Potato Patch Campground, phone (530) 258-2141
Information: Almanor Ranger District, Lassen National Forest, phone (530) 258-2141

Deer Creek Trail is the ultimate streamside path. It rises and falls gently, switching between grand views down on Deer Creek and intimate,

Lassen Peak from Manzanita Lake, late spring

shaded scenes beside this pleasantly noisy stream. You'll always be just a stone's throw away from constant rapids, small waterfalls, long cascades, and at one point, a large cataract. Trout anglers will find several side trails to the creek's banks—the fishing season is late spring through fall and Deer Creek is stocked with rainbow and brook trout nearly every week. Although the creek is crystal clear and full year-round, white water dominates in winter (when there's light snow at times) and spring. Maximize your experience by staying overnight at one of the numerous good campsites. This trail is also open to horses.

From Chester on Highway 36, drive west 12 miles to Highway 32. Drive another 12 miles southwest on Highway 32 and park on the left side of the road. From Chico, drive 40 miles northeast on Highway 32 and park 100 feet past the big Deer Creek bridge. Potato Patch Campground is a mere 1.7 miles north of the trailhead on Highway 32.

To begin, cross the northwest side of the highway and find the yard-wide dirt trail next to the Deer Creek Trail sign. The trail stays mostly level beneath Douglas fir, canyon live oak, incense cedar, and ponderosa pine. Farther on, a few black oaks and dogwoods enhance the landscape, turning to orange and red in the fall. Just past a small cave on the right, look for small California nutmeg trees, identified by sharp, dark green needles. Cross two streams full of moss-covered rocks and reach a clearing on a slope at 1.3 miles. Note the clusters of redbuds and continue to a precious view of a creamy white cascade surging over slick rock slabs. The trail crests then descends, first passing ceanothus and manzanita shrubs, and then canyon live oak.

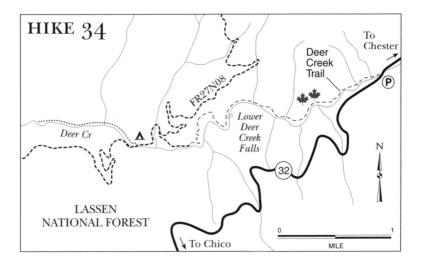

Lower Deer Creek Falls, spring

Be sure to explore all three spur trails at 1.6 miles that descend promptly to the Lower Deer Creek Falls area. The first path ends at a tremendous boulder perch overlooking the 15-foot-long and -wide falls. White water explodes against the large boulders and leaves a refreshing mist in your face. A small rock diversion dam also forms a chute here. The second path reaches a prime picnic spot, where various outcrops overlooking the falls offer photo opportunities galore. A third trail reveals scenic stretches of rushing rapids and swiftly moving water on its way west to the Ishi Wilderness and eventually the Sacramento River.

Continue on the main trail, staring at the lush and steep canyon walls that stretch some 800 feet above. Pass several campsites. Then climb through fragrant California bay laurel and enjoy more superb views of the canyon. Descend to Deer Creek and turn around at 2.3 miles, or continue downstream to Forest Road 27N08, a primitive campground, and more creekside hiking beyond.

SACRAMENTO VICINITY

35 § BEAR RIVER TO BEAR FALLS

Distance: 2-mile loop
Difficulty: Easy
High point: 1800 feet
Elevation gain: 50 feet
Map: Tahoe National Forest map, phone (916) 265-4531
Nearest campground: Beals Point Campground, phone (530) 988-0205
Information: Placer County Parks Division, phone (530) 889-7750

Every river features its own nuances and traits. This short excursion along the normally smooth-flowing waters of Bear River and up Osita Creek to modest Bear Falls is filled with wonder. You pass alder and willow near riverside, wander into tiny meadows, stroll past exposed chaparral, and meander beneath quiet and pristine forest. Come in late winter or early spring and feel the power of a swollen river surging urgently against its banks. Osita Creek is full and fast then, with a bevy of cascades below an active Bear Falls. The region is just as remote in autumn, when the river flows lazily and peacefully, and the oaks and maples change to vibrant colors. Hikers share the trail with horses.

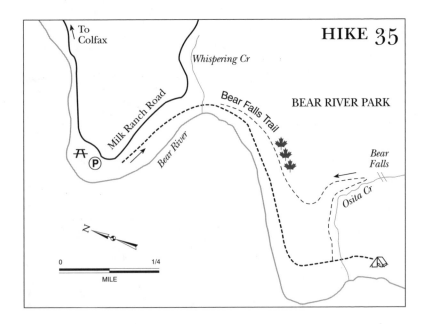

Bear River, early autumn

From I-80 at Colfax, 16 miles east of Auburn, take the Colfax/ Grass Valley Road exit. Turn right onto Auburn Road after going over the freeway, and then turn left onto Grass Valley Road. Turn left on Risingsun, and then left again onto Tokayana Way. After 0.7 mile, turn right onto paved Milk Ranch Road and drive 2.4 miles. Park in the large gravel parking lot at the picnic area.

Follow the wide, dirt service road past the green gate, and enjoy level strolling near shallow and clear Bear River. With a mix of steady currents and modest rapids, the 20-yard-wide river gently meanders past alders and gravel bars laced with willows. Most of the trail is shaded, courtesy of bigleaf maples, Douglas firs, and canyon live oaks.

Pass a trail on the left that is your return route. Within 0.5 mile, fragrant California bay laurel shows up along the U-shaped canyon, accompanied by occasional buckeye, redbud, and coffeeberry shrubs. Reach a pebbly flat at 0.8 mile where the native vegetation abruptly switches to ponderosa pine and black oak trees with an understory of ceanothus and manzanita chaparral. Cross a small meadow, reach the walk-in campground, and then bear left on a slender foot trail just past the second bathroom.

Slim Osita Creek is a steady murmur the entire 0.25 mile to Bear Falls and is virtually within spitting distance the whole way. The trail escorts you past a series of cascades that in late winter and early spring rush over a grayish brown rockbed. Once at the falls, cross the large log to stand beneath the 20-foot-high vertical rock wall that Bear Falls topples over. The falls, created from an overflowing ditch above the ledge, become a mere series of drips by early autumn.

Bear Falls Trail continues in dense woods where California grape frequently festoons ponderosa pines and Douglas firs. It reunites with the service road close to Bear River just before reaching the trailhead.

36 🍃 SOUTH FORK YUBA RIVER: PURDON CROSSING

Distance: 7 miles round trip
Difficulty: Easy to moderate
High point: 2200 feet
Elevation gain: 300 feet
Map: Tahoe National Forest map, phone (916) 265-4531
Nearest campground: Malakoff Diggins State Historic Park, phone (530) 265-2740
Information: South Yuba River State Park, phone (530) 432-2546

The hike along this stretch of the South Fork Yuba River is wild, remote, and powerful, set in a steep canyon that rises majestically and sports a scenic mosaic of dense oaks and erratic rock outcrops. You'll have numerous chances to hop on a huge boulder or sit on a bank of sand, watch the river flow, and space out. Swimming holes and good fishing abound and you'll probably not see a soul in the winter. In midautumn, dogwoods, black oaks, and bigleaf maples change to brilliant colors along the recently built South Yuba Trail.

From the interchange of Highways 20 and 49 in Nevada City, go west on Highway 49. After 0.4 mile, turn right on North Bloomfield Road, and then make a left 0.6 mile farther onto Purdon Road. After 3 winding miles, the road converts to a bumpy dirt road for 2.6 more miles, where you park just south of the bridge at Purdon Crossing.

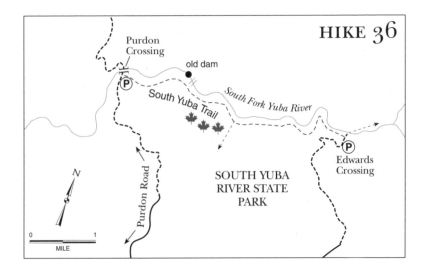

South Yuba River and Purdon Crossing, late spring

Before departing, examine the rustic, rusted steel bridge called Purdon Crossing, which was built in 1895 and used by miners. The narrow dirt path at first gently swings up the canyon, in a cool mixed forest of Douglas fir, incense cedar, canyon live oak, and bigleaf maple. Reach a fern-clogged babbling brook at 0.4 mile, where pipevine and wild grape form trellises on the trees.

Poison oak continues at trailside along with an impressive variety of native flora, including redbud, buckeye, black oak, toyon, California bay laurel, and a multitude of woodland perennial wildflowers. A spur trail at 0.7 mile leads down to the aquamarine waters of the South Fork Yuba River, which is a Class IV white water rafting run during high water in spring. Another side trail at 1.2 miles, beneath canyon oaks and pipevine, leads to a series of cascades that in spring rage over huge granite boulders. Heavy-duty climbing ensues over the next 0.7 mile, featuring a rewarding payoff of superb and extensive views down on swiftly charging South Fork Yuba River.

At 2.2 miles, cross two shaded seasonal streams profusely decorated by dogwoods, and then climb to a signed trail junction beneath a cluster of black oaks and bear left. Sun-worshipping ponderosa pines promptly join the high canopy, followed by ongoing views of the stark, south-facing canyon visage across the river. Note the abrupt change of terrain along this opposite slope, where clusters of gray pines nestle among dark brown boulder outcrops.

The shade gradually decreases as you gently descend past mountain misery ground cover to a reunion with the South Fork Yuba River at Edwards Crossing (3.5 miles). To continue hiking, cross the bridge here and keep heading up the river. ▪

37 🌿 COVERED BRIDGE TO ENGLEBRIGHT LAKE

Distance: 3.2-mile loop
Difficulty: Easy to moderate
High point: 750 feet
Elevation gain: 400 feet
Map: U.S. Army Corps of Engineers, phone (530) 865-4781
Nearest campground: Malakoff Diggins State Historic Park, phone (530) 265-2740
Information: South Yuba River State Park, phone (530) 432-2546

Stand on what is considered the most remarkable covered bridge in the United States, and then follow the wide and pretty final stretch of the South Fork Yuba River as it climaxes into dammed Englebright Lake. The trail overlooks the river's numerous beaches and gravel bars all the way to this slender, curving lake. Tucked into a modestly steep canyon in the scenic Sierra foothills, this is wild land where the

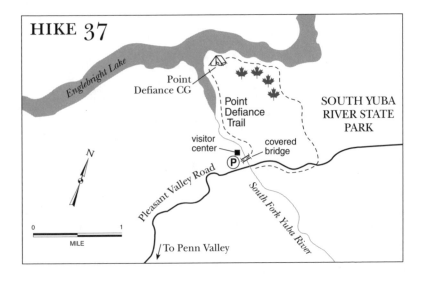

Covered bridge and South Fork Yuba River, spring

western fence lizard darts, the bobcat and mountain lion prowl, and the wild turkeys hide. Look for geese and canvasback ducks cruising the lake in early spring, and quail scurrying in the bushes during winter. In the fall, admire the colorful display of bigleaf maples, black oaks, and cottonwoods.

From Highway 20 in Penn Valley (east of Yuba City and west of Grass Valley), take Pleasant Valley Road north. After 7.9 paved and scenic miles, park in the large lot next to the visitor center and the old covered bridge.

Start by crossing the covered Bridgeport Bridge, which was built in 1862 and is quite unique. At 243 feet, it's the longest covered bridge left in the world and one of just a dozen in California. The arches and trusses have been protected from deterioration by the bridge's shake roof. While crossing this covered bridge, peer through the window slots to gaze upon a calm and wide stretch of aquamarine South Fork Yuba River.

The slender Point Defiance Trail promptly leads to a small sandy beach offering an ideal view of the covered bridge, as well as chances to wade and swim during warm spring and fall days. The dirt path then climbs gently in an interior live oak canyon, with occasional orange bush monkeyflower, styrax, and toyon shrubs at trailside. Next to a small madrone tree at 0.5 mile, reach a spur trail that leads to a large gravel beach flanked by tall Fremont cottonwoods. Another side trail 0.2 mile farther accesses a large and gorgeous sandy beach with a view of South Fork Yuba River's final swirls before its gradual transition into Englebright Lake. The trail overlooks Point Defiance Campground at 1.2 miles and then promptly drops to a wide spur trail that goes past willows to the confluence of the river and lake. The main trail veers east, featuring intimate views down on sea green Englebright Lake, framed by bigleaf maples, black oaks, and buckeye trees.

The way soon climbs, becoming a dirt fire road at 1.6 miles. After some heavy duty climbing, get views of the Yuba River Canyon, revealing tall gray pines casting scant shade over live oaks and blue oaks that cloak the steep canyon above the far shore. Check along the roadbed for boulders that jut out from the hillside—some of them have veins of quartz in the granite, once primary sources of gold.

38 ⚘ NORTH FORK AMERICAN RIVER AND POINTED ROCKS

Distance: 5-mile loop
Difficulty: Strenuous
High point: 1600 feet
Elevation gain: 1000 feet
Map: Auburn State Recreation Area map
Nearest campground: Beals Point Campground, phone (530) 988-0205
Information: Auburn State Recreation Area, phone (530) 885-4527

The North Fork American River is known for gold mining and whitewater rafting. It's rough and scenic with boulder banks, raging rapids, and deep blue pools. You'll be treated to photogenic views down on this swiftly flowing river, with no dams or diversions upstream. Rocky cliffs offer ideal launching pads for thrill seekers to jump from various heights into clear and cool pools. Then head directly up the canyon, way up. You'll be wheezing, but the payoff is rugged seclusion; some small but bizarre looking outcrops called Pointed Rocks; and views down into the canyon, across oak and pine foothills, and far away to the Sierra Nevada. Be sure to bring plenty of water and note that you'll share the trail with horses.

From Auburn on I-80, take Highway 49 east for 3.3 miles to the junction with Old Foresthill Road. Stay right and promptly cross the bridge over the North Fork American River. Park immediately on the right a few yards past the gate.

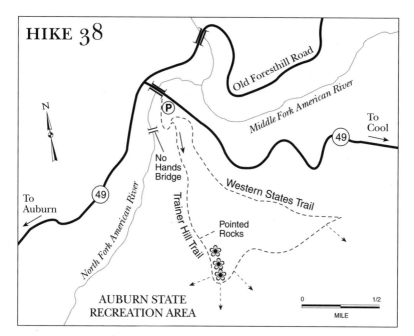

HIKE 38

To Auburn

To Cool

No Hands Bridge

Trainer Hill Trail

Old Foresthill Road

Middle Fork American River

North Fork American River

Western States Trail

Pointed Rocks

AUBURN STATE
RECREATION AREA

0 — 1/2
MILE

A dirt service road (no vehicles allowed) leads 200 yards to historic No Hands Bridge. After you've checked out the steep canyon and gazed some 100 feet down into the river from this bridge, double back to the bridge entry. Get on the slender and unsigned dirt path (Trainer Hill Trail) which reaches two Y-junctions. Bear right at each junction.

Climbing ensues at 0.2 mile on a wide phone-service dirt road past whiteleaf manzanita and two species of ceanothus to a view down on the river and a gravel bar. Traipse through a young, scattered forest dotted with ponderosa pine, knobcone pine, gray pine, interior live oak, and occasional Douglas fir. Moss-covered, oddly-shaped blue oak specimens mingle with pines at 1.1 miles as steep climbing continues. Reach the ridge top 0.4 mile farther, where toyon and coffeeberry in blue oak woodland form an isolated and western-movie-like landscape. Stay on the wide trail as it winds gracefully along a gentle, grassy grade where jackrabbits scurry and western fence lizards do push-ups.

Continue straight at a trail fork at 2.1 miles then reach several clusters of mostly chair-sized, lichen-coated boulders collectively called Pointed Rocks. About half of these rocks that are deeply embedded into the clay soil are somewhat pointed, hence the name. This is an ideal picnic spot. In winter and early spring, this small, oak-dotted meadow is lush green and you can see snow on the Sierras to the east. Native wildflowers abound here in March and April.

Continue onward, soon reaching Western States Trail at 2.3 miles. Turn left onto it, promptly pass another trail leading right, and continue straight. The path follows the ridge awhile, passing another trail that leads right, before descending along a more shaded canyonside. Views past ponderosa pines and Douglas firs are mostly of the distant Sierras and continue almost all the way to the trailhead.

A gray pine at North Fork American River, early autumn

39 FOLSOM LAKE AND MORMON ISLAND DAM

Distance: 13 miles round trip
Difficulty: Easy
High point: 500 feet
Elevation gain: 400 feet
Map: USGS Folsom
Nearest campground: Beals Point Campground, phone (530) 988-0205
Information: Folsom Lake State Recreation Area, phone (530) 988-0205

Folsom Lake was created in 1955, when the American River was dammed by Folsom Dam and its dikes. It's best for hikers to wait their turn to explore some of the 75 miles of the lake's shoreline. From May through September (the wrong time), the lake is an incessant buzz of motorboats, the weather is hot, and grasses are either overgrown or full of stickers along parts of the dusty trail.

The other months offer ideal off-season hiking, when on some weekdays the lake seems deserted except for you and the occasional red-tailed hawks, kestrels, and eagles that soar over the lake. This shoreline excursion allows you to admire the lake when the waters recede so low in late autumn that big boats can't embark. In winter, when new annual grasses are cheery green and low, watch for Canada geese

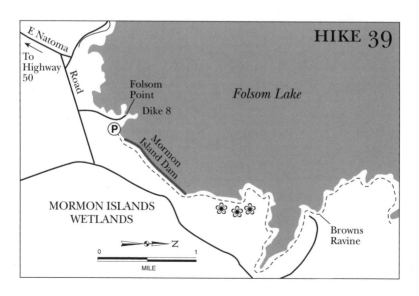

Folsom Lake, early spring

cruising the lake. By late winter, foothill animals tend to come out of hiding more often since there are fewer people around. If you're quiet and lucky, maybe you'll see a bobcat or raccoon at twilight.

From Highway 50 in Sacramento, take Folsom Boulevard north for 2.8 miles. Turn right on East Natoma Road and drive 3.1 miles. Then turn north on the paved road signed for Folsom Point. Continue 0.7 mile to the picnic area and beach.

The trail snakes around a small cove choked with partially submerged willows. Traipse along Mormon Island Dam, the mile-long Dike 8 Trail, where you can focus on sailboats gliding across the dark gray waters of 18,000-acre Folsom Lake. Gaze upon a sea of cheery yellow green as immense cottonwoods and willows occupy much of protected Mormon Island Wetlands to the southeast. Bring binoculars to search out small birds year-round and to view several kinds of larger birds that migrate here in late autumn and early winter.

Follow the contour of the rocky shoreline past the leaning and twisted trunks of gray pines and blue oaks with toyons stashed beneath. Pick up a slender footpath near a cozy inlet clogged with willows at 1.5 miles. Clover, lupine, and vetch (all legumes) are in peak flowering stage here in late April and early May. Note how the poison oak grows as a ground cover, a shrub, and a vine creeping up some of the interior live oaks along a dense wooded stretch. Look for a grove of handsome buckeye trees just before reaching this hike's largest cove. Watch for duck families paddling near the shore just before reaching the waterfront docks at 2.2 miles. The trail vanishes here, but reappears farther along the shore, where it continues for miles.

40 COSUMNES RIVER PRESERVE

Distance: 3-mile loop
Difficulty: Easy
High point: 200 feet
Elevation gain: 50 feet
Map: Cosumnes River Nature Trail map
Nearest campground: Beals Point Campground, phone (530) 988-0205
Information: Cosumnes River Preserve, phone (916) 684-2816

The marshes and sloughs of Cosumnes River Preserve are precious jewels tucked surprisingly close to an otherwise plain stretch of I-5. Travel through some of the finest valley oak groves found anywhere

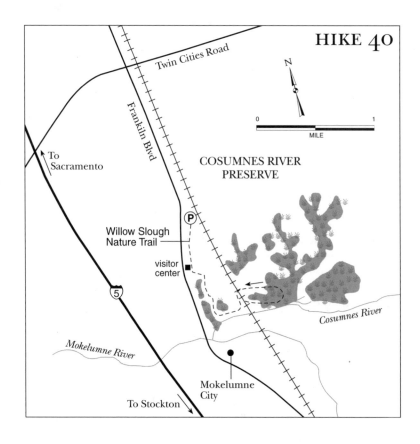

Pond at Cosumnes River Preserve, midspring

and enjoy this unique bird paradise, with the Cosumnes River on one side of you and marshes and sloughs on the other. In winter, the Cosumnes River floods adjacent fields and creates seasonal freshwater marshes, which attract huge flocks of migratory waterfowl. More than 200 species of birds have been spotted here, including the threatened sandhill cranes and Swainson's hawks. Migratory songbirds such as northern orioles and yellow warblers breed on the preserve. Native perennial grasses are cheery green in winter, and wildflowers burst into bloom in early spring. After heavy rains, flooding can transform trail portions into slush, although several wood bridges cross the worst parts. Call ahead for the latest conditions and bring your own water. Pick up a map from the visitor center or from the trailhead dispenser.

From I-5 some 14 miles south of Sacramento's southern outskirts, take the Twin Cities exit and head east. After 1.2 miles, turn right onto Franklin Boulevard, drive 1.4 miles and park in the large gravel lot on the left.

Walk though a grove of young valley oaks (a successful oak restoration project) and reach some benches, where you can pick up the Willow Slough Nature Trail brochure from a dispenser for a fifty-cent donation. The trail soon narrows, passing by a willow slough and cutting through a meadow dominated by creeping wild rye, a native perennial grass that thrives in low lying areas subject to flooding.

A soothing transformation occurs as you duck briefly into a riparian forest of Oregon ash, black willow, and towering valley oak at 0.3 mile. The good trail skirts the edge of a buttonbush swamp to the west and a freshwater seasonal marsh to the east, which accompanies you for another 0.8 mile. Cattails dominate this expansive marsh, which is also home to western pond turtles and Pacific tree frogs.

The calm and muddy waters of the Cosumnes River greet you just beyond a grove of mighty valley oaks that stretches beyond a historic railroad bridge at 1.2 miles. Pass under an interior live oak (post number 15), which oddly is the only live oak on this 14,000-acre preserve. The Willow Slough Nature Trail winds past a tule marsh lined with arroyo and yellow willows, and traipses through an open oak savanna featuring statuesque specimens to the north.

Note the numerous Fremont cottonwoods towering over willows clogging a slender marsh to the west just before reuniting with the railroad tracks at 1.8 miles. Yellow-billed magpies, unique to California's Central Valley, are commonly sighted near this railroad stretch along the savanna.

41 🌱 ANDERSON MARSH

Distance: 5 to 6.5 miles round trip
Difficulty: Easy
High Point: 1500 feet
Elevation gain: 300 feet
Maps: USGS Lower Lake, Clear Lake
Nearest campground: Ritchey Creek Campground, phone (707) 942-4575
Information: Anderson Marsh State Historical Park, phone (707) 994-0688

Uniquely beautiful oaks and a huge bird sanctuary are delightful highlights of this hike. Add to the mix a lot of photo opportunities and few folks, and this trip becomes a soul-satisfying adventure.

Winter is the best time for bird-watching, when abundant waterfowl covet rain-replenished Anderson Marsh. This expansive and curving marsh hosts slow-flapping pelicans, large great blue herons, precious green herons, elegant white snow geese, graceful egrets, quacking ducks, and plenty more. Just settle at a chosen perch, focus the binoculars and gasp when droves of free birds take to the sky over the

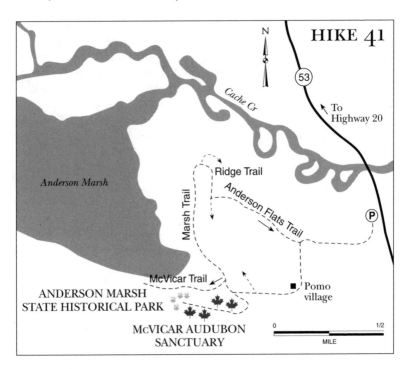

marsh. Early fall is usually the most comfortable time to explore, as the temperatures have cooled and you avoid the mud brought on by winter and spring rains. Nevertheless, wildflowers and cheerful green grasses adorning the oak woodlands above the marsh are a treat from late winter through midspring.

From the junction of Highways 53 and 20, 38 miles west of I-5 and just east of Clear Lake, travel south for 7 miles on Highway 53. Turn west into Anderson Marsh State Historical Park, 0.7 mile north of Highway 29.

To start, head west across a field for 0.4 mile and take a left at an unsigned trail junction. Continue alongside a chain-link fence past the occasional valley oak.

The trail then climbs beneath the dappled shade of blue oak and alongside greenleaf manzanita to a signed trail junction at 1.1 mile. Go left and suddenly spy sprawling Anderson Marsh. Cross the meadow, with willows and Fremont cottonwoods adorning the marsh shore on the right and scattered gray pines dominating the foothill on the left.

Enter an extra wet stretch of trail and soon approach the marsh shore. At 1.6 miles, spot the sign indicating McVicar Audubon Sanctuary, go left, and then climb 100 yards to a sloping walnut orchard. The trail skirts a lush stretch of redbud, elderberry, buckeye, and black oak, climbs to an enticing view of the marsh at 2 miles, and peters out. Retrace your steps to the marsh edge, and then head left on the McVicar Trail for ample bird-watching along a 0.7-mile-long moist and weedy trail.

When you've had enough, retrace your steps to the unsigned trail fork atop the hill, and go left at a rattlesnake sign onto Marsh Trail. This trail furnishes the most intimate views of the marsh as it skirts the eastern shoreline next to blue oaks for 0.7 mile. Admire the tall stand of valley oaks on the right, especially the lone giant ahead of you once you reach the Ridge Trail. Reach a bench beneath a massive valley oak with views to the northeast of the moist lowlands and the riparian habitat of Cache Creek. Turn left onto unsigned Anderson Flats Trail and head east for about 1 mile through an oak-studded meadow to the trailhead.

Blue oaks at Anderson Marsh, early autumn

SAN FRANCISCO BAY AREA TO BIG SUR

42 ⚘ RIDGE TRAIL TO PROSPECT TUNNEL

Distance: 9.5-mile figure-eight loop
Difficulty: Moderate to strenuous
High point: 1100 feet
Elevation gain: 1200 feet
Map: USGS Antioch South
Nearest campground: Bort Meadow Campground, phone (510)
  635-0135
Information: Black Diamond Mines Regional Preserve, East Bay
  Regional Park District, phone (510) 635-0135

It's hard to believe that more than a century ago, this wild and rugged foothill country was full of miners with picks carving out some 150 miles worth of coal mining tunnels. This hike takes you halfway into 400-foot long Prospect Tunnel (bring a flashlight with fresh batteries), and also covers jagged and jumbled ridges, erratically sloped grasslands, and sprawling valleys, all dotted with blue oaks and patches of chaparral. This is remote land where the prairie falcon soars and

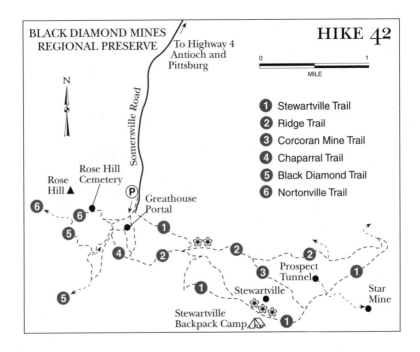

BLACK DIAMOND MINES
REGIONAL PRESERVE

To Highway 4
Antioch and
Pittsburg

HIKE 42

0 MILE 1

N

Somersville Road

Rose Hill ▲ Rose Hill Cemetery (P) Greathouse Portal

❶ Stewartville Trail
❷ Ridge Trail
❸ Corcoran Mine Trail
❹ Chaparral Trail
❺ Black Diamond Trail
❻ Nortonville Trail

Prospect Tunnel●

Stewartville

Star Mine

Stewartville Backpack Camp ⛺

the coyote still howls at night, out of sight and sound of cars and houses, though the trail is open to mountain bikers and horses. The numerous views of Mount Diablo and neighboring East Bay foothills are superb, and the native trees and shrubs are diverse, including the rare Coulter pine in its northernmost range. There is no water along the trail, so fill up at the faucet in the parking lot or bring your own.

From Highway 4 in Antioch (just east of Pittsburg), turn south onto paved Somersville Road. Continue straight after 1.6 miles (at the 10 mph sign) and proceed 2 narrow and winding miles to the large parking lot. Bort Meadow Campground is in nearby Anthony Chabot Regional Park. The signed Nortonville Trail (named for an old coal mining townsite) climbs gently 0.6 mile to small and peaceful Rose Hill Cemetery nestled at the base of Rose Hill. Decorated by cypress trees, it's a monument burial ground for those who died in mining disasters.

Loop left on signed Black Diamond Trail, ignore the first left then get on the Chaparral Loop Trail at 1.3 miles. This narrow path contrasts significantly with the spacious grassland you just left behind. Tall and stalwart manzanita shrubs, with their nonconformist, crooked branches, highlight this loop that alternates between short climbs and descents amid toyon, black sage, and shrubby forms of coast live oak. A mix of gray pines and Coulter pines (they have the largest cones of all pines) accentuate the landscape, which is more arid than other East Bay lands—this spot resembles the Sierra foothills.

Continue on Chaparral Loop Trail and bear left onto Lower Chaparral Loop Trail. There's a rocky gulch bottom with initials inscribed just before reaching the Greathouse Portal. Peer through the iron bars blocking the original entrance to this sand mine and observe the rectangular tunnel built from railroad ties. Sand was transported through this tunnel for glass making. Climb back to the top of the main Chaparral Loop Trail and check out the brush- and boulder-clogged knoll rising sharply above a thicket of tiny-leafed chamise shrubs.

Retrace your steps, climbing to Ridge Trail. Go left and enjoy views of the rocky knoll and the Rose Hill Cemetery you visited as well as calm Suisun Bay to the north. Ridge Trail eventually crests a ridge, revealing a soft scene of grassy hills leading to the flat and fertile farmlands of the Central Valley. Ridge Trail now drops into a gracefully sloping blue oak woodland sporting a gorgeous grove of large buckeye trees (lush white flowers in late spring) just below. Stay on Ridge Trail at a junction 3.2 miles into the trip, and commence another stealthy climb along a grassy slope, promptly offering a rare view of the northeast face of Mount Diablo.

Reach the signed Corcoran Mines Trail at 4 miles—taking it will shorten the trip by 2 miles. Otherwise continue down the Ridge Trail 400 feet in elevation through blue oak woodland. Veer sharply right onto the signed Stewartville Trail (also named for a coal mining townsite). You'll stay on this dirt path all the way to the trailhead. This old ranch road follows a broad valley that's glowing green in wintertime and then dotted with wildflowers in early spring. The trail stays close to a meandering seasonal stream for a good while. Then, at 6.3 miles, pass a huge buckeye tree and reach a three-way trail junction. A left turn heads 0.5 mile to Star Mine, a barrel tunnel used for coal mining. Go right for a side trip to Prospect Tunnel. Even without a light, there's enough sunlight to proceed several yards into the five-foot-wide and equally high chamber.

Mount Diablo from Ridge Trail, early autumn

Back on Stewartville Trail, you soon pass Corcoran Mile Trail, an old wooden corral, and then the backpack camp beneath a pair of extremely wide valley oak trees. The trail stays flat and follows another seasonal stream with admirable views of a steep ridge with imposing rock embedded in the steep cliff sections. At 7.7 miles, the trail veers 90 degrees to the right and climbs this ridge. Turn left at a fork with Miners Trail, cross Ridge Trail, and continue about 0.6 mile to your car.

43 COYOTE TRAIL AND BOB WALKER RIDGE

Distance: 6.2-mile loop
Difficulty: Moderate
High point: 1977 feet
Elevation gain: 800 feet
Map: USGS Tassajara
Nearest campground: Sunol Campground, phone (510) 635-0135
Information: Morgan Territory Regional Preserve, East Bay Regional Park District, phone (510) 635-0135

The best way to find solitude, jaw-dropping views, and gorgeous grand-daddy oaks is to take this hike into the East Bay's most remote region—Morgan Territory. Wonder no more about what's on the distant, seldom seen east side of prominent Mount Diablo. This hike features a series of high hills running north to south. From these ridge tops on a clear winter's day, the far off and snow clad Sierras resemble white caps way out to sea. Spring brings green slopes with profuse flashes of wildflowers such as buttercups, tidy tips, phacelias, and lupines. Visit in autumn to see the immense rock clusters embedded in the canyons and slopes punctuate the golden brown carpets of spent ranchland grasses. Get water from a parking lot faucet or bring your own.

Drive Ygnacio Valley Road from I-680 in Walnut Creek and turn right on Clayton Road. Make a right onto Marsh Creek Road, and then turn right after a couple of miles onto paved Morgan Territory Road. After 9.5 winding and shaded miles, turn left into the large parking lot at Morgan Territory Regional Preserve. From Livermore, take Highland Road to Morgan Territory Road.

Signed Coyote Trail, a narrow path, cuts through a swath of tall perennial bunchgrasses that wave gently in the wind. Moments afterward, you reach a dainty and colorful pond at a signed trail junction (stay left on the Coyote Trail). Beneath a distinctively shaped valley

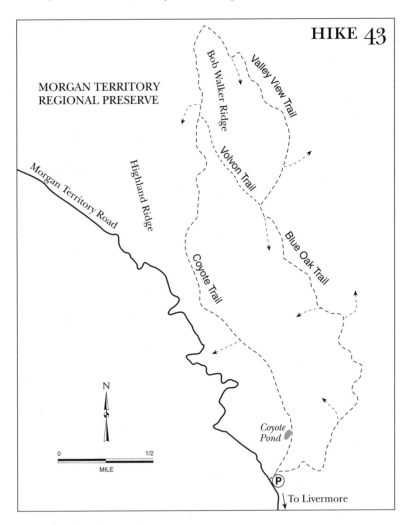

MORGAN TERRITORY
REGIONAL PRESERVE

HIKE 43

Bob Walker Ridge

Valley View Trail

Volvon Trail

Morgan Territory Road

Highland Ridge

Blue Oak Trail

Coyote Trail

N

0   1/2
MILE

Coyote
Pond

P

To Livermore

oak giant, admire this teardrop-shaped pond from a large and flat
boulder. Enter an evergreen hardwood forest of bay laurel and coast
live oak that's vibrant in the fall and winter. The reddish limbs of
thriving manzanita specimens (up to 14-feet high) sometimes intrude
on the trail alongside occasional ocean spray, toyon, poison oak, and
snowberry shrubs. Thick-roped California grape climbs bigleaf maples
at 0.7 mile, the junction of two seasonal streams at another signed
trail junction. Continue straight.

At 1 mile, enter a serene setting where a rocky-bottomed seasonal stream continues gradually downhill past a valley oak with a monster trunk. Soon Coyote Trail meanders on the outskirts of open grassland and promptly takes you under a magnificent pair of giant buckeye trees (white flowers in late spring). The climbing proceeds gently, revealing an impressive array of stand-alone blue oaks with unique trunk shapes and branching patterns. Coyote Trail becomes a compacted dirt road at 1.5 miles. Bear right and look west to admire a photogenic view of Highland Ridge as you continue to climb. There are two things to marvel over while ascending the grassy ridge—dark but bright green leaves of coast live oak contrast wonderfully with the grayish green leaves of blue oaks, and these giant blue oaks are some of the biggest you will ever see.

Pass a dinky cow pond, and then reach a pass and a trail junction at 2.2 miles. A right turn here on the Volvon Trail makes this a nice 4.4-mile loop hike. For the longer hike, continue north, climbing gradually over grassland and around Bob Walker Ridge.Quickly scamper up to its crest to sit on one of the many lichen-coated boulder perches to cherish westward views of Highland Ridge and eastward scenes of fertile farmlands and the Sierras. At 2.9 miles, bear left onto Valley View Trail for numerous eastward views down on the flat-as-an-ocean Central Valley and beyond to the distant Sierras.

Valley View Trail passes a junction with Manzanita Trail to the left and meets Volvon Trail at 4.1 miles. Go left for less than 0.1 mile and then turn left on the signed Blue Oak Trail to enjoy countless specimens of blue oaks blessed with age and character. Southward views now appear of lonely, rolling hillsides like the one you're on. Stay on Blue Oak Trail until you reach the parking lot in a little over 2 miles.

Coast live oak from Bob Walker Ridge, early autumn

44 🌿 MOUNT DIABLO'S BACK AND MITCHELL CANYONS

Distance: 15-mile loop to Mount Diablo; 8.6-mile loop to Murchio Gap
Difficulty: Moderate to strenuous
High point: 2350 feet; 3849 feet
Elevation gain: 1900 feet; 3300 feet
Map: USGS Clayton
Nearest campground: Live Oak Campground, phone (925) 837-2525
Information: Mount Diablo State Park, phone (925) 837-2525

Get a real feel for the Bay Area's most seen and perhaps most spectacular mountain with a varied hike loaded with breathtaking views of seemingly endless East Bay hills. The trail climbs the north face of Mount Diablo, wanders into flower-strewn (in spring) meadows and grassland, explores narrow Back and Mitchell Canyons, and reveals several far-reaching, sunswept panoramas of Northern California. The tiny stream in secluded Back Canyon pours over and between sensational eroded rock, and the whole journey displays a tremendous variety of native shrubs, trees, and flowers. Make sure to carry a lot of water and note that you may encounter horses along the way.

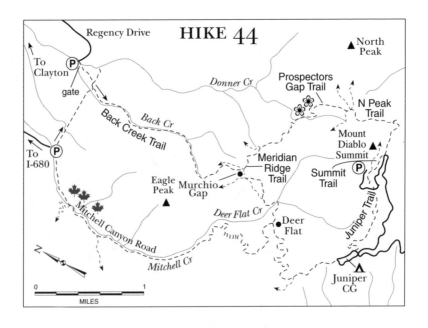

Near Murchio Gap, late autumn

From I-680 in Walnut Creek, take the Ygnacio Valley Road exit and drive east for 7.8 miles. Bear right onto Clayton Road, travel 2.8 miles, and then turn right onto Regency Drive and continue 0.5 mile to its dead end. After descending an embankment and crossing the park gate, take a right at the dirt road fork, which leaves the side of Donner Creek. Walk past oat grass and randomly spread valley oaks. Then bear right at an unsigned road fork and promptly left at another unsigned trail junction.

Slender Back Creek flows below the trail, framed by buckeye, blue oak, interior live oak, and gray pine for the first 0.5 mile. Cross a gate and continue past orange bush monkeyflower, fragrant sage, toyon, and yarrow. A bit farther, several spur trails break to the left amid chamise, wild grape, poison oak, and yerba santa; always stay right to climb Back Canyon, which steepens at 1.3 miles. From 2.1 to 3.2 miles, chamise dominates, interspersed with yerba santa and eventually thickets of whiteleaf manzanita recovering from a major fire that ravaged this area in 1977.

Upon reaching isolated Murchio Gap at 3.5 miles, there's the option for fit folks (or patient hikers who have all day) to climb another 1500 feet to Mount Diablo's summit. Just head left on Meridian Ridge Trail, which climbs to Prospectors Gap (this main dirt road becomes Prospectors Gap Trail). Climb past bay laurel, blue oak, live oak, poppy (spring), and lupine (spring) to North Peak Trail, which becomes Summit Trail and promptly climbs to the top of Mount Diablo. From the summit, the photogenic panorama encompasses more square miles than any other view in the United States. Descend via Juniper Trail past large bay laurel and gray pines to the campground, and then follow the trail 1.7 miles down to Deer Flat. This view-filled stretch shows off shrubby yellow aster, lupine, brodiaea, chamise, ceanothus, and occasional elderberry, canopied by scattered blue oaks and gray pines.

If you choose to bypass the summit, head south from Murchio Gap on either trail 0.8 mile to Deer Flat, which sports two picnic tables. It's also the most abundant wildlife and birding area in the park. Admire the views of Mount Diablo's summit to the southeast, Eagle Peak to the northeast, and East Bay to the west. Bear right here and adore these views while going down 1 mile to gently swirling Mitchell Creek. Reach a grassy flat where canyon oaks and coast live oaks grow magnificently tall near creekside.

Follow alder- and bigleaf-maple-lined Mitchell Creek for 2.4 miles, keeping to the right on the fire road (Mitchell Canyon Road). This trail passes through grasslands featuring Coulter and gray pines to reunite with the trailhead.

45 ⚘ PINE RIDGE: PINE CANYON LOOP

Distance: 8.5 miles round trip
Difficulty: Moderate to strenuous
High Point: 1800 feet
Elevation gain: 2000 feet
Map: USGS Diablo
Nearest campground: Live Oak Campground, phone (925) 837-2525
Information: Mount Diablo State Park, phone (925) 837-2525

The labyrinth of Mount Diablo's foothills are inviting doorsteps, laced with an impressive variety of native plants and wildlife. This ramble up Pine Canyon and along Pine Ridge is a wide open door revealing intimate views of the mighty mountain proper, along with countless scenes of striking woodland and creekside landscapes. There are photo opportunities of nearby East Bay hillsides and close-up studies of a rock city consisting of sandstone outcrops. Hikers share the trail with horses and the hike is dry, so bring plenty of your own water.

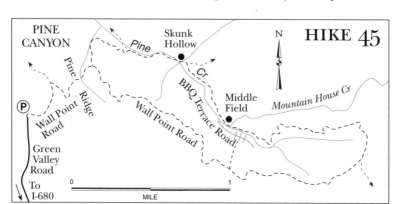

From I-680 just south of Walnut Creek, take the Stone Valley Road east exit. Drive 3 miles and turn left onto Green Valley Road. Proceed 1.2 miles to the large parking lot.

From the parking lot, follow Wall Point Road some 400 feet in elevation over smoothly sloping grassland. The Briones-Mount Diablo Trail soon cuts left, but you continue on Wall Point Road to the right. The widely scattered coast live oak and valley oak trees are shapely and stately, and soon you're treated to views of the poshest neighborhood imaginable, a fairy-tale-like scene of fantastic castlelike dwellings capped by the distinguished backdrop of Las Trampas Ridge.

Arguably the best head-on views of Mount Diablo are attained in a flat where you soon bear left at a trail junction and proceed into a blue oak and gray pine woodland, dotted with coast live oak and occasional madrone trees. This mostly flat trail section meanders quietly above a seasonal offshoot of Pine Creek, cozily decorated by yellow buttercups in early spring.

After 0.5 mile, the trail gets up close and personal with Pine Creek, following it closely over its very gentle rise next to serviceberry shrubs, beneath bigleaf maples, and alongside an oak savanna. Cross a feeder stream at Skunk Hollow. Continue straight at a signed trail junction onto Barbecue Terrace Road. Climb to a flat laden with valley oak giants and soon reach Middle Field at 3.2 miles. This is an ideal picnic site, strewn with large boulders and shaded by huge buckeye, California bay laurel, bigleaf maple, and coast live oak trees.

After a 0.3-mile climb out of Middle Field, a connector footpath to the right leads promptly to a cute little cascade (winter and spring only), and then marches up a narrow and oak-clothed woodland

Sandstone formations along Wall Point Trail, early autumn

canyon. Take this trail to shorten the trip by 2 miles and 400 feet of climbing. Otherwise bear left at the signed trail junction, climb the grassland slope, capture far-reaching views of the East Bay foothills and Mount Diablo, and stay right at the next three trail junctions. Get on Wall Point Road at 5.2 miles.

The remainder of the journey is a leisurely return mainly on a sunny high ridge section of the Wall Point Trail. First, there are clusters of unique sandstone rock formations and abundant views. Then tough, native shrubs take center stage, including chamise, sage, bush lupine, and poison oak.

46 ABRIGO VALLEY AND MOTT PEAK

Distance: 6.3-mile loop
Difficulty: Moderate
High point: 1424 feet
Elevation gain: 900 feet
Map: USGS Briones Valley
Nearest campground: Bort Meadow Campground, phone (510) 635-0135
Information: Briones Regional Park, East Bay Regional Park District, phone (510) 635-0135

Get lost in a daydream while wandering in a spacious sanctuary of broad valleys and smoothed ridges on this hike laden with ponds and

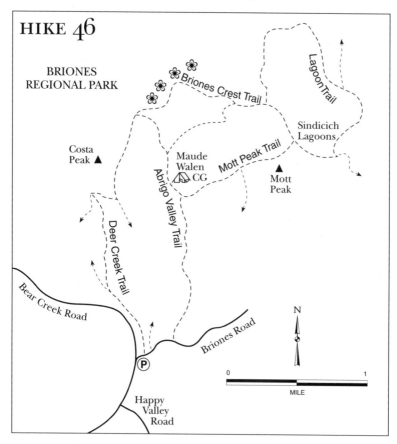

HIKE 46

BRIONES
REGIONAL PARK

Briones Crest Trail

Lagoon Trail

Costa
Peak ▲

Maude
Walen
⛺ CG

Abrigo Valley Trail

Mott Peak Trail

Sindicich
Lagoons

Mott
Peak ▲

Deer Creek Trail

Bear Creek Road

Briones Road

N

P

0 ——————— 1
MILE

Happy
Valley
Road

spectacular views. Briones Regional Park is one of the most remote, largest, and least visited parks in the East Bay. Wildflowers abound in the spring, and, in autumn, the thick forests become dappled in browns and yellows, especially where the bigleaf maples grow in the valleys. Share the trail with mountain bikers and horses.

From Highway 24 east of the Caldecott Tunnel, take the Happy Valley Road exit. Go east on El Nido Ranch Road, and then north on Upper Happy Valley Road. After 1 mile, turn left onto paved Happy Valley Road and drive for 2 miles. Turn right onto paved Bear Creek Road, drive 0.3 mile, and turn right into Briones Regional Park. Park in the large lot at Oak Grove.

Signed Deer Creek Trail passes a small pond then heads into a wide valley surrounded by a unique mix of cone-shaped grassy knolls and dense hardwood forest hills. At 0.5 mile, pass an algae-lined pond with tall spikes of sedges, and then head into cozy Deer Creek Canyon. The California bay laurel trees reach uncommonly prodigious heights and widths along the borders of the narrowing creek, dwarfing the willows. An 80-foot wide laurel, with a large bathroom-sized trunk drapes its fragrant leaves over the trail at 1 mile. A modest climb ensues up and out of the canyon, lined with ancient coast live oaks. The climb is eased by views down into the Deer Creek Canyon.

Follow Deer Creek Trail as it angles right, and then reach an oval pond at a pass (1.5 miles) and turn left onto the Briones Crest Trail. Be sure to make a side climb of a grassy knob called Costa Peak, an ideal perch for admiring the Bay Area, including Mount Diablo to the east and Mission Peak to the southeast. The constantly curving Briones Crest Trail furnishes 1.5 miles of intimate views of gracefully sloped hills and broad Abrigo Valley. At 2.8 miles, you can abbreviate the trip by 3 miles if you bear right onto signed Abrigo Valley Trail.

The main hike continues briefly on Briones Crest Trail and then loops left and clockwise onto Lagoon Trail. Take in scenes of Suisun Bay and Mount Diablo, look down into brushy Toyon Canyon (at about 4 miles), and eventually wind up at Sindicich Lagoons at 4.7 miles. The largest of these ponds features a nice, curving outline, with a handful of distinguished willow trees decorating the shoreline. Hang a right at the trail junction, look back down on Sindicich Lagoons with Mount Diablo in the background, and then turn left 0.3 mile farther onto the Mott Peak Trail. It's a quick climb to grassy Mott Peak to admire previously mentioned views plus Briones Peak to the east.

Sindicich Lagoons and Mount Diablo, early autumn

An old dirt ranch road, Mott Peak Trail soon drops steeply alongside a hardwood forest mainly of coast live oak and bay laurel to Maude Walen Camp at 5.2 miles. The final mile down the Abrigo Valley Trail is a pleasant and scenic stroll. Red-tailed hawks screech above the tree canopy searching hungrily for mischievous squirrels that chirp playfully on the valley edge.

47 ⚘ ROUND TOP AND VOLCANIC TRAIL

Distance: 4.2-mile loop
Difficulty: Easy to moderate
High point: 1763 feet
Elevation gain: 700 feet
Map: USGS Briones Valley
Nearest campground: Bort Meadow Campground, phone (510) 635-0135
Information: Sibley Volcanic Regional Preserve, East Bay Regional Park District, phone (510) 635-0135

Look closely and you will see volcanic dikes, lava flows, and mudflows on this hike. The self-guided trail system (grab a handy brochure at the trailhead dispenser) leads to and beyond Round Top, an extinct volcano that dispersed its lava 9 million years ago. An ideal stomping ground for geologists (they've counted eleven separate lava flows), the preserve has a complicated geological and local history as well as an unpredictable future. Exotic grasslands, native chaparral, and native hardwoods are thriving here along with introduced eucalyptus. This landscape contrasts sharply with neighboring Huckleberry Botanic Regional Preserve, an ecological jewel with native plants found nowhere else in the East Bay. Catch decent views of the East Bay and San Francisco Bay, but the real views are from a couple of special spots where a hiker truly feels on top of the world. These perches reveal breathtaking views of the Diablo Range and closer Las Trampas Ridge to the east. You may encounter horses on the trail.

From Highway 24 northeast of Oakland, drive just east of the Caldecott Tunnel. Take the Fish Ranch Road exit west, which loops 1 mile to Grizzly Peak Boulevard. Turn left and drive 2.5 miles to Skyline Boulevard. Turn left, go 100 yards, and then turn left into the large Sibley Volcanic Regional Preserve parking lot.

Take the footpath near the drinking fountain, and walk through

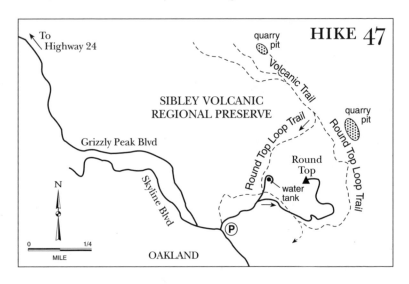

a unique forest of non-native Monterey pines and eucalyptus growing alongside native coyote brush, toyon, and coffeeberry. This habitat combination attracts great horned owls and golden eagles. Turn right at the signed junction of the paved trails and climb 1763-foot-tall Round Top in 0.7 mile. Although the views are okay from up here, better views follow farther on.

Descend Round Top and bear left on the narrow Round Top Loop Trail at 1.3 miles. Soon reach sloping grassland followed by a quarry pit, which exposes the interior of Round Top volcano. Round Top Loop Trail turns off to the left—this is your return route—but continue straight on the Volcanic Trail for better views and interesting geologic formations.

There are three trails near the 2.2-mile point. First take the lower left trail and drop to a clearing, and then to a rim with a badly eroded cliff face. The view down the canyon reveals an interesting contrast—grass on the west facing slope and dense trees and shrubs on the east facing slope. The soil hosting the trees and shrubs has better fertility and development. Retrace your steps to the Volcanic Trail. Turn left and follow it to a red-baked sequence of air-fall tuffs and a basalt lava flow (both are described in the park brochure). Double back again, this time taking the upper trail left to a quarry pit and a set of thick lava flows tilted on edge, nearly vertical.

Plan on spending quality time at this major quarry pit, the deepest and steepest of the hike. Take the spur trail on the left for an exceptional view of the pit's stark cliff face with Mount Diablo rising to the east. Note the chiseled and weathered appearance of the thick lava flows on the north wall, with a bake zone at the base. Finish climbing the spur trail to a knoll for a splendid view of San Francisco, the Bay Bridge, and the bay. Another side trail enables you to look down on the quarry while getting sprawling views of rolling hills to the north. Note the strange thicket of bay laurel atop a knob of scattered boulders. Perch yourself on one of these large lava boulders and look up into the twisted trunks of the large laurels.

Mount Diablo from quarry pit, late autumn

48 🌿 BORT MEADOW AND BUCKEYE TRAIL TO GRASS VALLEY

Distance: 6.2 miles
Difficulty: Easy to moderate
High point: 1500 feet
Elevation gain: 900 feet
Map: USGS Las Trampas Ridge
Nearest campground: Bort Meadow Campground, phone (510) 635-0135
Information: Anthony Chabot Regional Park, East Bay Regional Park District, phone (510) 635-0135

This hike comprises an equal mix of grassland, hardwood forest, and brush, spread out leisurely and making an ideal wildlife environment. Eucalyptus- and redwood-ringed Bort Meadow is a lush grassland full of frolicking kids on sunny weekends, and is an inviting start for this hike. Grass Valley caps the journey, virtually unrecognizable as a grassy valley since native trees and shrubs, such as fast-spreading coyote brush, have taken over much of it. In between, quiet creek walking and divine views of nearby canyons and ridges punctuate the trip with pleasing variety. This hike is not a page-turning thriller, but is more like a mellow read at night that sends you into a satisfying sleep. Mountain bikers and horseback riders also use this trail.

From I-580 in Oakland, take the 35th Avenue exit and drive east (it soon becomes Redwood Road). Pass Skyline Boulevard and Pinehurst Road and drive 1.8 miles farther. Park on the right in the

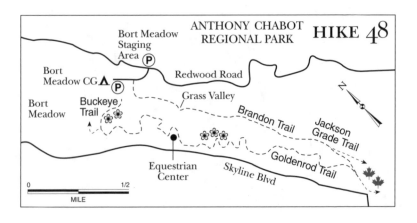

signed lot or in Bort Meadow Campground. From Castro Valley, Redwood Road heads north and reaches the parking lot in a few miles.

To start, pick up Buckeye Trail at the west end of Bort Meadow. This herb-bordered footpath climbs gently along a serene seasonal stream, shaded by madrones, coast live oak, and buckeye trees with a sculpted look, their massive and leaning branches coated with moss. Irish green in early spring, this short trail section glistens with ferns, moss, and lush foliage. Serviceberry shrubs neighbor cow parsnips, which join miner's lettuce as one of the primary native smaller plants.

After 0.6 mile, ascend wooden steps and turn left onto an old dirt

Goldenrod Trail, early autumn

road called Goldenrod Trail. This trail climbs past a water storage tank beneath huge eucalyptus and pine trees, becomes paved briefly, and then suddenly shows off inspiring views of the rolling hills to the east. Snake through an upper canyon portion, densely clothed in an impressive variety of native vegetation. The sunny sections are full of bush lupine (purple flowers in early spring), orange bush monkeyflower, coyote brush, and California sage. The primarily shaded parts are home to fragrant California bay laurel, coast live oak, toyon, elderberry, and some tall and handsome Monterey pine trees.

At 3.1 miles, a half mile past the Equestrian Center, you reach this hike's highest elevation featuring sprawling views of south San Francisco Bay to the west (cross Skyline Boulevard for better photographs) and far-reaching scenes to the southeast of eucalyptus groves and power lines (pretend they're not there). As the Goldenrod Trail veers left and down at a trail junction at 3.6 miles, it passes by tremendous stands of sky-high eucalyptus trees, with trunks only as thick as telephone poles and spaced a mere few feet apart.

A modest stand of small redwoods and some bigleaf maples highlight the brief descent on the Jackson Grade Trail. When you reach the creek, dart left onto Brandon Trail, which promptly leads to a bench shaded by a grand bigleaf maple and some more redwoods within peaceful earshot of the creek. This flat dirt road is noticeably and refreshingly tranquil, and follows the straight course of the willow-clogged creek amidst occasional alders, coast live oak, and California bay laurel. Before starting your return trip, reward yourself by dawdling in serene Grass Valley across the creek.

49 🌿 OLIVE AND THERMALITO TRAIL LOOP

Distance: 7.9-mile loop; 2 miles round trip to ridge top
Difficulty: Moderate
High point: 1573 feet
Elevation gain: 1500 feet
Map: USGS Dublin
Nearest campground: Bort Meadow Campground, phone (510) 635-0135
Information: Pleasanton Ridge Regional Park, East Bay Regional Park District, phone (510) 635-0135

The graceful, nonconformist habit of the distinguished coast live oak is best appreciated as a stand-alone specimen along a sweeping grassy slope or a remote ridge top. This is the recurring scene on this view-filled hike, which explores deep canyons and ridgetop vistas adorned with some of Northern California's most majestic coast live oak giants. The rural atmosphere has been deliberately preserved as perhaps it was ages ago, with gorgeous groves of century-old olive trees currently being restored.

Most of the sandstone and cobble gravels that form the rocks of Pleasanton Ridge derive from up to 70-million-year-old eroded marine formations deposited in the inland Pacific Ocean. In fact, fossils from marine-dwelling snails, clams, oysters, and sand dollars are still discovered here. Turkey vultures, red-tailed hawks, and occasionally golden eagles watch smaller birds, such as western bluebirds and meadowlarks that dart over the grasslands full of ground squirrels, alligator lizards, and western fence lizards. You may encounter cattle along the way, and the trail is open to mountain bikers and horses. As with most Bay Area hikes, fall, winter, and spring visits avoid summer haze and people.

From I-680 near Pleasanton, take the Bernal Avenue exit and drive west for 0.2 mile. Turn left (south) on Foothill Road and continue 3.2 miles to the large dirt parking lot.

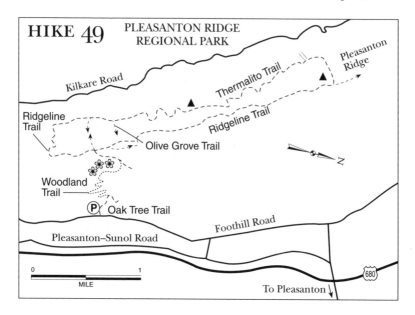

HIKE 49 — PLEASANTON RIDGE REGIONAL PARK

The signed Oak Tree Trail, an old dirt road, climbs from the parking lot and winds past magnificent gargantuan poison oak to a signed trail junction with the Woodland Trail at 0.2 mile. Bear left near a couple of towering crooked-trunked coast live oak giants and continue climbing. Soon, ancient valley oak trees with randomly draping limbs alternate with open grassland that is awash with low-growing, violet-colored filaree annuals in early spring.

After 1.2 miles of sprawling views to the east, featuring Mount Diablo and its neighboring foothills, arrive at the Ridgeline Trail and the hike's first evergreen orchard of ancient olive trees adorning the plateau. Go right along the Ridgeline Trail, another old dirt road; the steady hum of I-680 traffic noise below is replaced by the often soothing whistle of a salty sea breeze.

Bear left at 1.5 mile for a brief side trip past statuesque olive trees (continue straight and soon reunite with Ridgeline Trail). Continue straight at the trail junction next to a seasonal pond, and then traipse through the middle of a final grove. Have your camera ready for great shots of the pond framed by the olive trees and Mount Hamilton in the distance. Climb the knob just to the north, which reveals a larger pond (potential home to the western pond turtle, chorus frog, and the threatened California red-legged frog) and a panorama of East Bay foothills.

Pleasanton Ridge, spring

The Ridgeline Trail continues its gentle ascent to a globed crest at 3.2 miles where you bear left onto Thermalito Trail (the return loop). This trail displays commanding vistas into a densely wooded canyon, passes a tiny and narrow waterfall that pours from a seasonal pond in winter and spring, and eventually reunites with signed Ridgeline Trail at almost 6 miles. Bear left and walk 0.7 mile to regain Woodland Trail. Turn right and return to your car.

50 ZEILE CREEK AND GARIN PEAK

Distance: 5.8-mile loop
Difficulty: Easy to moderate
High point: 948 feet
Elevation gain: 800 feet
Map: USGS Hayward
Nearest campground: Sunol Campground, phone (510) 635-0135
Information: Garin Regional Park, East Bay Regional Park District, phone (510) 635-0135

Roam these rolling cattle ranchlands and be close to thriving wildlife while snagging sweeping views of the East Bay and neighboring Hayward Hills. Granted, these aren't jaw-dropping vistas, but they're refreshingly mellow. Native trees and shrubs line reclusive Zeile Creek, and you may spot the gregarious ground squirrel leading its typically public life there or anywhere on this varied journey. When you come, hike to the ridge, and then sit, wait, and look downslope for a chance sighting of the keen coyote or alert fox. This hike explores an ordinary yet wonderful section of typical East Bay ranchland, typified by the lush winter cover of filaree, a pretty annual associated with cattle. Mountain bikers and horses also use this trail.

From I-880 in Hayward, take the Tennyson Road exit east to Mission Boulevard. Turn right and soon turn left onto Garin Avenue, where you climb almost 1 mile to the large parking lot.

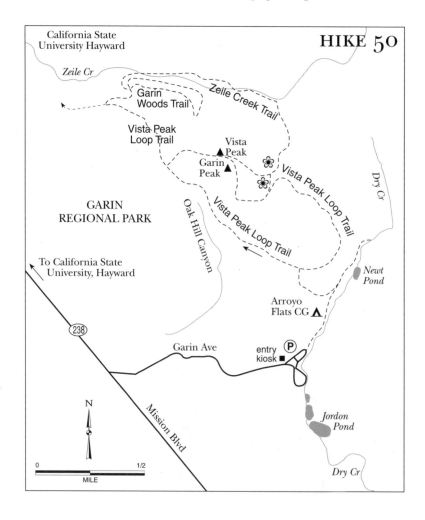

From the far north parking area, leave the grand California sycamore trees, an impressive mixed orchard, and the large barn, which serves as the visitor center and has ranching artifacts on display. Stroll along a seasonal stream to Arroyo Flats (a group camp). Bear right at 0.2 mile where two dirt ranch roads join for a brief scamper to willow-lined Newt Pond. In late winter and early spring, this small, spring-fed cattail marsh is heavily populated with croaking frogs and cute newts.

Retrace your steps to the group camp, then bear right onto the Vista Peak Loop Trail, which promptly starts a moderate 600-foot climb to the ridge. First pass an old corral. Then go left at a trail junction at 0.8 mile. As the trail skirts around a large, smooth and rounded knoll, sneak previews unfold of the East Bay, framed by a trio of deformed willows and large eucalyptus triplets. On a moonless evening, the city lights give off a moody glow here.

At 1.5 miles, note Garin and Vista Peaks to the northeast. They are readily accessible from the signed trail on the right. If depleted of time and/or energy, take this trail now. Otherwise continue straight to a pass yielding a backdoor view of California State University, Hayward. These smooth slopes are a rich green carpet in winter and early spring, and gradually dry into a yellow and brown blend of spent grasses that shine in the late afternoon sun in autumn.

Follow the trail down, turning right onto Zeile Creek Trail. Garin Woods Trail soon takes off to the right through dense hardwood forest, making a short loop (go either way). Northern exposure provides the shade and moisture needed to support hardwoods. Winds along this trail are mainly buffeted by California bay laurel and coast live oak, but occasional black oak, canyon live oak, madrone, gooseberry, and hazelnut also provide wind breaks. Return to Zeile Creek Trail at 2.4 miles and go right. Follow this year-round creek for a good

Vista Peak Loop Trail, autumn

0.3 mile, mainly past willows and laurel, as it veers south and heads up a wooded canyon.

You soon climb to a grassy pass at the junction with Vista Peak Loop Trail at 3 miles. Turn right to reach 934-foot-high Vista Peak and its neighbor, 948-foot-high Garin Peak. These two bare knobs are virtually identical, so choose just one and get rewarded with expansive East Bay views along with scenes of Mission Peak dominating the Fremont Hills to the south. Note that many of the nearby peaks are accentuated by distinctive coast live oaks that add a touch of beauty and uniqueness to the scenery. In midspring, these peaks are dotted with native wildflowers such as California poppy, mule ears, and Indian paintbrush. Retrace your steps to the trail junction and continue right on the loop trail to return 1.3 miles to the trailhead.

51 ❦ RED HILL AND NORTH MARSH

Distance: 6.4-mile loop
Difficulty: Easy to moderate
High point: 400 feet
Elevation gain: 500 feet
Map: USGS Newark
Nearest campground: Bort Meadow Campground, phone (510) 635-0135
Information: Coyote Hills Regional Park, East Bay Regional Park District, phone (510) 795-9385 or (510) 635-0135

Rich in history, Coyote Hills Regional Park features a mix of trails offering a variety of scenic sites. This hike covers the key highlights, including a chance to sniff the south San Francisco Bay breezes while taking in the views from atop Red Hill. Wander along Alameda Creek and imagine where on its banks the Ohlone Indians had their cluster of dome-shaped tule houses a couple of centuries ago. Walk through large freshwater and saltwater marshes and watch for sandpipers racing over the mudflats and herons and egrets tiptoeing along the salt ponds.

In the winter, this wildlife sanctuary is brisk with birds, and by springtime, there's a raucous chorus of croaking frogs. Muskrats maintain the marshes with their ravenous appetite for roots. Fall is the best time for clear views, and people are scarce in winter. Stop by the visitor center for the naturalist program or the informative historical exhibits. You may encounter mountain bikers and horses along the trail.

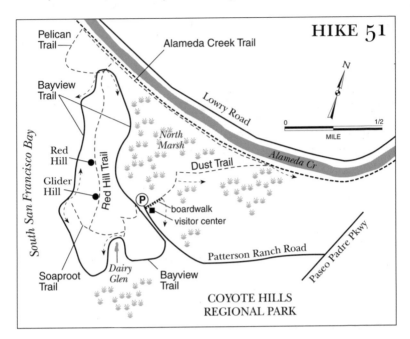

From Highway 84 westbound in Fremont, take the Paseo Padre Parkway exit. Turn north, and then turn right onto paved Patterson Ranch Road for the final mile to the large Coyote Hills Regional Park parking lot. If coming from I-880, take the Thornton Avenue exit, follow this road around until it becomes Paseo Padre Parkway, and then follow the signs to the park. Bort Meadow Campground is in nearby Anthony Chabot Regional Park.

From the visitor center, head briefly south, climb a flight of railroad ties, and then scramble up a two-story-high boulder for a condor's-eye view of North Marsh. Descend to paved Bayview Trail. Turn right and walk halfway around Dairy Glen pond. Partially retrace your steps, and then head west (left) on a dirt road called Soaproot Trail. Turn left at the signed junction to climb an unnamed hill. From this grassy knob, enjoy close-at-hand sweeping views of the South Bay, Dumbarton Bridge, and Dairy Glen pond. Follow the Soaproot Trail west 0.3 mile to the junction with Bayview Trail and a bench that serves as another vantage point for soaking up bay views.

Retrace your steps up Soaproot Trail, turn left on Red Hill Trail then huff and puff up to Glider Hill at 2.2 miles, where daredevils hang-glide. Drop down, and then march up Red Hill for a commanding panorama of previously mentioned views plus Oakland to the north and mighty Mission Peak standing guard over the Fremont Hills to the east.

The Red Hill Trail climbs another panoramic knob, traverses through a wild garden of licorice-scented fennel, and then descends to Bayview Trail at 3.1 miles. Go left a few steps and then turn right onto Pelican Trail. Wander west along a slender peninsula to experience South Bay up close. The trail finishes on the south bank of Alameda Creek at 4.2 miles. Turn right and walk east on a narrow and flat cinder track alongside the bike trail and admire gradually curving Alameda Creek as it flows gently toward the rolling Fremont Hills. The grayish and relatively deep creek averages about 25 yards in width and is bordered on both banks by cattails and algae.

Expansive North Marsh soon appears on the right, featuring a nice view of a curvaceous pond backed by Red Hill. After 1 mile, make a sharp right onto a dirt road called Dust Trail, which proceeds along the shore of a long and skinny pond. Within 0.5 mile, you're smack dab in the middle of North Marsh. A jungle of cattails taller than you wave in the wind—it's like being deep in the Florida Everglades, but without the gators and crocodiles. Wintertime affords the most solitude, and you will see more birds than in other seasons. The mile-long trail finishes by crossing the boardwalk, which leads to the parking lot.

South San Francisco Bay from Red Hill, spring

52 ⚮ ROSE PEAK AND MURIETTA FALLS

Distance: 20 miles round trip; 11.5 miles round trip to Murietta Falls
Difficulty: Strenuous
High point: 3817 feet; 3300 feet
Elevation gain: 4300 feet; 3500 feet
Map: USGS Mendenhall Springs
Nearest campground: Del Valle Regional Park, phone (925) 373-0332
Information: Del Valle Regional Park, East Bay Regional Park
District, phone (510) 635-0135

The Bay Area's longest waterfall, second tallest peak, and most won-drous oak trees beckon on this view-filled journey into highly isolated Ohlone Regional Wilderness. Getting to little-known and hidden Murietta Falls, named after the legendary 1800s outlaw Joaquin Murietta, will cause even fit hikers to be a little stiff and sore the next day. Climbing up and down the two ridges to the falls on a hot, dry day is like an extreme sport. There is no water along the ridge and you will need it. Bring at least two quarts per person per day.

On a clear day (most likely in autumn), there are several vantage points (especially from Rose Peak) for jaw-dropping views of the Sierra, Mount Whitney, Mount Hamilton, the Santa Cruz Mountains, and San Francisco and its bay. Sometimes in winter, the oak-dotted peaks and ridges above 3000 feet are lightly glazed with snow. January through April is the best time to enjoy the falls before the roar is reduced to a trickle and then eventually vanishes sometime in the summer. Plan for an extra long day hike if headed for Rose Peak, or stay overnight at one of the backcountry campsites to make the trip more leisurely. Horses and their riders also use this trail.

From Livermore on I-580, take the North Livermore Avenue exit and travel south on this road (which becomes Tesla Road). After 3.8 miles, turn right on paved Mines Road. Then go right again 3.6 miles farther on paved Del Valle Road. Follow it for another 3 miles, cross the bridge, and continue to where the road dead-ends at the camp-ground parking lot.

Get on Vallecitos Trail, a yard-wide footpath for most of its 1-mile climb, and pass scattered stands of bay laurel, coast live oak, and gray pine above patches of miner's lettuce. The views of the Livermore foothills and Lake Del Valle improve soon after going left on the Ohlone Regional Wilderness Trail, which you stay on at all signed

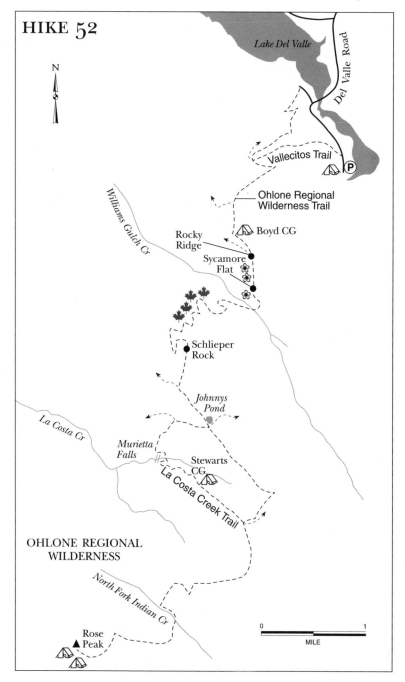

HIKE 52

N

Lake Del Valle

Del Valle Road

Vallecitos Trail

P

Ohlone Regional
Wilderness Trail

Boyd CG

Williams Gulch Cr

Rocky
Ridge

Sycamore
Flat

Schlieper
Rock

Johnnys
Pond

La Costa Cr

Murietta
Falls

Stewarts
CG

La Costa Creek Trail

OHLONE REGIONAL
WILDERNESS

North Fork Indian Cr

Rose
Peak

0   1
MILE

junctions over the next 3.5 miles. The persistent climb steepens noticeably in spots, traversing upper hills and canyonsides laced with a wide variety of chaparral, which contrasts greatly with the naked Livermore hills across Del Valle. Modest-sized gray pines and blue oaks poke above the native shrubs of coyote brush, sagebrush, black sage, and toyon, later joined by coffeeberry and chamise.

After climbing 1600 feet in elevation from the trailhead, reach the crest of Rocky Ridge at 2.3 miles alongside a pair of huge blue oaks with crooked limbs. In early spring, this flat and grassy expanse is dotted with yellow Johnny-jump-ups and pinkish purple shooting star flowers. The old ranch road descends to fittingly named Sycamore Flat at 2.7 miles, where a trio of tall, native western sycamores displays showy white trunks. The trail begins to narrow at some buckeye trees bordering Williams Gulch Creek, a scenic picnic spot.

A hefty 1200-foot climb ensues through black oak woodland interspersed with buckeyes and bay laurels. At 4.2 miles, scamper up cottage-sized, lichen-coated Schlieper Rock for commanding views to the north and east. Now an old ranch road again, Ohlone Regional Wilderness Trail climbs past a couple of clusters of valley oaks festooned with mistletoe—some oak specimens are stunted with grotesque growths.

Views abound from the ridge top, which leads to Johnnys Pond at 4.7 miles, nestled in a clearing. From the west side of this small pond, get on the dirt ranch road that leads past several strikingly gorgeous rock formations down to a broad, U-shaped grassy valley. Turn left onto La Costa Creek Trail (also known as Greenside Trail), cross the free-flowing creek that offers cute little cascades making their way to Murietta Falls, and then follow a dry spur trail to the lip of the falls. To get to the foot of the falls, negotiate the spur trail around an array of rock outcrops and then down to a small, rocky pool at the base of slender Murietta Falls. They plunge some 100 feet over slick gray rock. The sun begins to light up the falls by late afternoon, enhancing the scene's stark contrast—wild falls are a surprise in this sprawling grassland and oak habitat.

Retrace your steps back up to La Costa Creek Trail. If energy and time permit, start a modest climb past Stewarts Camp at 6 miles to reunite with the Ohlone Regional Wilderness Trail 0.5 mile farther. Though miles away, Rose Peak soon comes into view as you stroll toward it along this wild and scenic ridge top. Supreme vistas keep unfolding, past North Fork Indian Creek at 8.5 miles and at last, to the tippy top of 3817-foot-tall Rose Peak, which is just a few feet lower than Mount Diablo. Stay overnight at designated campsites below the peak and climb less than 1 mile in the morning to catch a gorgeous sunrise.

Murietta Falls, early spring

53 MONUMENT PEAK

Distance: 8-mile loop
Difficulty: Moderate to strenuous
High point: 2594 feet
Elevation gain: 2500 feet
Maps: USGS Calaveras Reservoir, Milpitas
Nearest campground: Joseph D. Grant County Park, phone (408) 274-6121
Information: Ed R. Levin County Park, phone (408) 262-6980

Of the three major peaks that stand guard over the Santa Clara Valley (Mount Hamilton and Mission Peak are the other two), Monument Peak is the most overlooked but the most secluded. This hike climbs steep and grassy slopes sparsely dotted with coast live oaks to a series of peaks atop a ridge called Monument Peak. The views of the San Francisco Bay are far-reaching and fantastic for 90 percent of the hike, with a myriad of connector trails and side paths leading to the top.

This trip offers variety by passing into a number of canyon bottoms laden with mature native oak, sycamore, and bay trees. Come in the fall for the best chance of good views and a possible encounter with a male tarantula spider crossing the trail looking for a mate. The hills are so open and expansive, you might look down on a wily coyote or a smart fox on the hunt. Red-tailed hawks cruise the ravines and hilltops for their meals and comprise one of more than sixty-four bird species found in the park. Note that hikers share the trail with horses.

From I-680 or I-880 in Milpitas, take the Calaveras Road exit and follow this road east a few miles to Ed R. Levin County Park. Turn left onto paved Downing Road, which promptly passes the park entrance kiosk and Sandy Wool Lake. The trailhead and parking lot are on the northeast side of the lake.

To start, climb east out of the foothill valley that was formed by millions of years of plate movement along the Calaveras and Hayward faults. The ascent begins immediately on Tularcitos Trail, one of this hike's many old dirt ranching roads. You'll be wheezing like a donkey during the steep climb, so pause often to look down on willow-lined Sandy Wool Lake and the salt marshes of San Francisco Bay.

Turn left onto Agua Caliente Trail and soon after, pass through a colony of licorice-scented fennel at 0.8 mile. Reach a slender creek at 1.4 miles, bordered by gigantic California sycamore and California

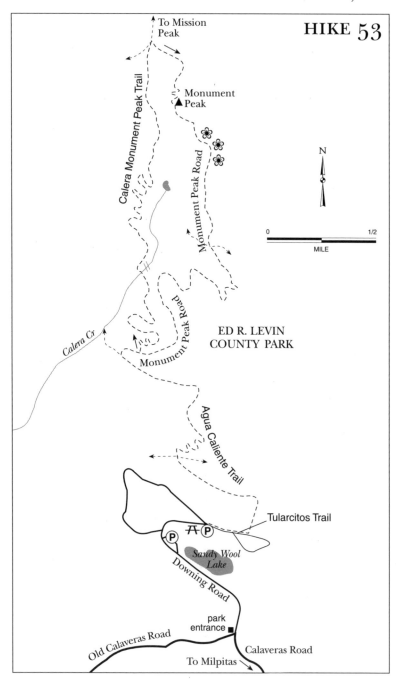

HIKE 53

To Mission Peak

Calera Monument Peak Trail

Monument Peak

Monument Peak Road

N

0 ___ 1/2
MILE

Calera Cr

Monument Peak Road

ED R. LEVIN COUNTY PARK

Agua Caliente Trail

Tularcitos Trail

P   A   P

Sandy Wool Lake

Downing Road

park entrance

Old Calaveras Road

Calaveras Road

To Milpitas

Eastward view from Monument Peak, early autumn

bay laurel. Turn right on the signed Monument Peak Road 0.3 mile farther, and climb to a fascinating coast live oak featuring several abnormally thick lower limbs leaning horizontally. At 2.1 miles, cross a pretty section of Calera Creek where a modest but delightful waterfall tumbles on the right and two towering sycamores display huge, twisted multiple trunks on the left.

After another 1.5 miles of sweating and heavy breathing, you reach a trail junction. A left turn heads 2 mostly flat miles north to Mission Peak, which has transmitters on it, like Monument Peak. Our hike goes right and soon reaches Monument Peak at 4.2 miles, where the best views now are to the east of Mount Hamilton and Calaveras Reservoir. Note the interesting boulder outcrops and rock fence at Monument Peak.

54 ⚘ CHINA HOLE AND WILLOW RIDGE

Distance: 26-mile loop
Difficulty: Moderate to strenuous
High point: 2700 feet
Elevation gain: 4800 feet
Maps: USGS Mississippi Creek, Mount Sizer; Henry W. Coe State Park map
Nearest campground: Henry W. Coe State Park, phone (209) 826-1196
Information: Henry W. Coe State Park, phone (408) 779-2728

Enjoy a backpack trip wandering along scenic oak savanna, grassy canyon bottoms, and gently sculpted foothills in an isolated and pristine land loaded with special views of slopes, canyons, and wild creeks. Admire an impressive array of native trees and shrubs that often grow to uncommonly tall heights and huge girths. By midautumn, the bigleaf maples, sycamores, willows, and alders display their peak fall colors along Coyote Creek and its east fork. During a cold spell in winter, your feet will be crunching frost and ice in the sheltered canyon bottoms. After heavy winter rains, Coyote Creek swells power-fully, making crossings risky (call ahead). Come March, there are spec-tacular displays of wildflowers such as buttercups, shooting stars, and popcorn flowers, especially along Willow Ridge Trail and Mahoney Meadows. Trails along this route are also open to horses.

Drive US 101 to Morgan Hill, south of San Jose, and take the East Dunne Avenue exit. This paved road climbs and twists 12.5 miles to the Henry W. Coe State Park Visitor Center.

Begin by taking the signed Corral Trail and soon reach a clearing featuring a gigantic valley oak decorated with profuse mistletoe. Head right 50 yards farther onto signed Springs Trail at 0.4 mile. This 2-mile-long trail passes two springs then continues along an open hilltop offering sweeping vistas of steep hills through a savanna dotted with coast live oak, black oak, valley oak, and blue oak. Watch for an attractive third spring at 1.7 miles, lined with native rushes. Soon after, reach a multisigned trail junction and go straight onto the Coit Route dirt road.

You'll soon reach a bass pond at 2.1 miles and another nearby where a spur loop trail leads to Manzanita Group Camp. At 2.5 miles,

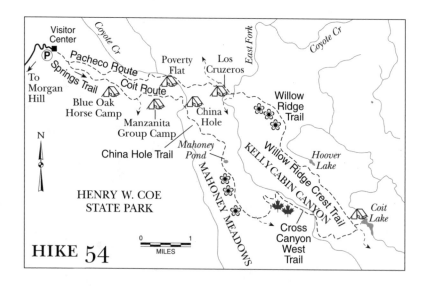

continue straight at a signed trail junction onto the China Hole Trail, and descend past big berry manzanita, black oak, and ponderosa pine, followed by chamise and blue oak. Eventually come to China Hole, which doubles as a swimming hole and a trout fishing spot, with campsites near Coyote Creek.

Continue to Mahoney Pond and Mahoney Meadows along Mahoney Ridge on a walk through oak savanna that curves past tall gray pines. Check out views to the west of gorgeous Coyote Creek Canyon and scenes of Blue Ridge, Pine Ridge, and Middle Ridge to the northwest. Descend 1 mile along Cross Canyon West Trail past ceanothus, ocean spray, and huge big berry manzanita specimens. The fall colors are fantastic. Some black oak and madrone show up near the canyon bottom.

On the floor of Kelly Cabin Canyon, the trail veers abruptly southeast and follows a seasonal creek past coast live oak, sycamore, bay laurel, and bigleaf maple. The trail leaves the creek after 1 mile and ascends several side canyons to the signed junction with Willow Ridge Crest Trail (a dirt road) where you go left. A spur trail to the right soon heads east to Coit Lake, which is loaded with bass and offers good swimming and camping.

Back on Willow Ridge Crest Trail, pass shallow Hoover Lake and sections of chamise chaparral as you admire previously mentioned views to the north and west as well as the Pacheco drainage to the east. Go left, staying on Willow Ridge Trail 3.5 miles after Coit Lake, and then descend 1000 feet in 1.3 miles to the East Fork Coyote Creek. Los Cruzeros, another backpack camp, is just downstream. Cross the creek and continue on the Pacheco Route past Poverty Flat to the visitor center 3 miles farther.

Valley oak at Mahoney Meadows, early winter

55 ⚘ CREAMERY MEADOW AND PANORAMA TRAIL

Distance: 8-mile loop; 2.4-mile loop to Molera Beach
Difficulty: Moderate to strenuous
High point: 1100 feet
Elevation gain: 1100 feet
Maps: USGS Point Sur, Big Sur
Nearest campground: Andrew Molera State Park, phone (831) 624-7195
Information: Andrew Molera State Park, phone (831) 624-7195

From the moment you enter Creamery Meadow en route to Molera Beach and eventually some high bluffs, you'll be smack dab in a bird paradise. Look for the belted kingfisher and the three-foot-tall great blue heron swooping over Big Sur River and the western seagull or black and white willets searching sandy Molera Beach for food. Climb beyond the bluffs via fittingly named Panorama Trail while the red-tailed hawk soars above.

This amazing journey displays a blanket of oat and barley grasses dotted with poppies and wild mustard in Creamery Meadow during spring. A good 5 miles of the hike feature sweeping views of rolling hills and incessant waves crashing against steep and stark bluffs. Come in autumn for the best visibility.

Drive 21 miles south of Carmel on Highway 1 to the Andrew Molera State Park entrance. Turn right into the parking lot.

Start by veering right onto Beach Trail at a small, sandy beach lined with willows along the swirling Big Sur River. The primitive campground is 400 yards along the wide and sandy trail. The way soon enters Creamery Meadow, a hodgepodge of grasses and patches of bush lupine and coyote brush. You get to stroll for almost a mile between this meadow and the river's edge, in an ultimate locale for spying wildlife, from deer and birds to boars. Majestic sycamores and occasional Fremont cottonwood trees tower over willow and blackberry thickets that line the riverbanks, with a splendid view of rolling oak hills to the east alongside a large gravel bar.

At 1.2 miles, a cluster of driftwood forts and noisy waves rinsing slender Molera Beach caps the scene where Big Sur River empties into the sea. A pair of big boulders make good perches during low or midtide. While strolling the beach, note the purple patterns in the sand, caused by almandite dissolving in the nearby cliffs.

The Bluffs Trail offers the best roosts for intimately admiring the shoreline. This sandy and mostly flat path keeps guard over the steep bluffs' edges most of its 2-mile course, highlighted in spring by yellow-flowered bush lupines. Bluffs Trail passes through tall perennial bunchgrasses and coyote brush, offering just one access to Molera Beach—curvy Spring Trail. At 2.8 miles it drops from Bluffs Trail to a secluded and scenic portion of Molera Beach, which disappears at high tide. Grand views galore continue from the bluffs, especially of Franciscan Rocks to the north and numerous pocket beaches in both directions.

Cross a second gully and get set to start puffing like a steam locomotive on the invigorating 1100-foot climb along the mile-long Panorama Trail. The sweating and swearing is soon replaced by encompassing views of oak hills, sea stacks, Molera Beach, and other sites, further proving Andrew Molera State Park is tops in panoramas in the Monterey/Big Sur area.

The trail loops around and becomes Ridge Trail at 4.4 miles. More superb lookouts follow, as ancient coast live oaks take center stage

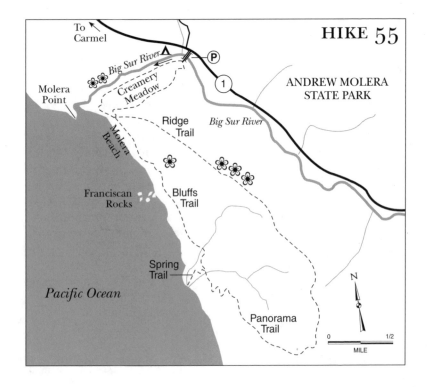

Molera Beach, winter

along the first part of this dirt fire road. Low-growing coastal scrub of coast sage, coyote brush, and orange bush monkeyflower adorn the trailside, accentuating the views. Atop Molera Point to the north, a threesome of statuesque Monterey cypress trees appears as a serene silhouette come twilight. Point Sur Light Station can be seen further north, anchored atop a massive volcanic rock. Before the lighthouse was built in 1889, this rugged area experienced several disastrous shipwrecks.

At 7 miles, look down on Creamery Meadow and the Big Sur River. Then descend to the south loop (go right) that borders the meadow and soon reaches the trailhead.

56 ❦ POINT LOBOS

Distance: 6.5-mile loop
Difficulty: Easy
High point: 200 feet
Elevation gain: 500 feet
Map: USGS Soberanes Point
Nearest campground: Pfeiffer Big Sur State Park, phone (831) 667-2315
Information: Point Lobos State Reserve, phone (831) 624-4909

Experience highlight heaven by exploring the rocky shoreline of Point Lobos, renowned for its irregular coves, brazen headlands, soft

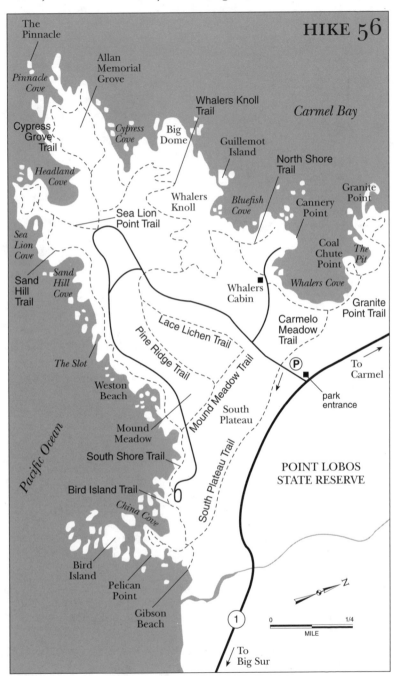

HIKE 56

The Pinnacle

Pinnacle Cove

Allan Memorial Grove

Carmel Bay

Whalers Knoll Trail

Cypress Grove Trail

Cypress Cove

Big Dome

Guillemot Island

North Shore Trail

Granite Point

Headland Cove

Whalers Knoll

Bluefish Cove

Cannery Point

Sea Lion Point Trail

Sea Lion Cove

Coal Chute Point

The Pit

Sand Hill Trail

Sand Hill Cove

Whalers Cove

Whalers Cabin

Granite Point Trail

Carmelo Meadow Trail

Lace Lichen Trail

Pine Ridge Trail

The Slot

Mound Meadow Trail

(P)

park entrance

To Carmel

Weston Beach

South Plateau

Pacific Ocean

Mound Meadow

South Shore Trail

South Plateau Trail

POINT LOBOS STATE RESERVE

Bird Island Trail

China Cove

Bird Island

Pelican Point

Gibson Beach

N

1

0   1/4
MILE

To Big Sur

meadows, and pristine beaches. It took millions of years for nature to create this varied and scenic seaside, a fascinating interaction between sea and land that typifies Point Lobos. This excursion traces the perimeter of Point Lobos in clockwise fashion, featuring intimate encounters with several beaches and coves that contrast strikingly with each other. As added bonuses, you'll capture far-reaching views of the ocean and check out extremely rare natural stands of native conifers. Other attractions include barking sea lions basking on Sea Lion Rocks and southern sea otters sleeping motionlessly, resembling dark floating logs mingled in the brown seaweed.

Autumn is the best time for the best views and weather. Winter is a time when there are the fewest visitors to this popular place. In spring, when the breezes kick up, the small meadows are green and awash with wildflowers.

Drive 4 miles south of Carmel on Highway 1 and turn right into the Point Lobos State Reserve.

Begin on level and needle-littered South Plateau Trail, which is shaded by native Monterey pines and a few coast live oaks. The understory includes orange bush monkeyflower, blue blossom ceanothus, coffeeberry, and poison oak that often climbs high into the pines. At 0.8 mile, there is a three-way junction. Wooden steps descend to the left to the spacious white sands of Gibson Beach. A good loop trail leads straight to a ledge overlooking Bird Island. This steep rock knob is often covered with Brandts cormorant seabirds. The South Shore Trail heads right around Point Lobos.

Reach China Cove at 1.3 miles. It's coated with shimmering white sand bordering clear and calm aquamarine water and a two-way sea tunnel. Back on South Shore Trail, come upon a small, rock-encased pocket beach called Hidden Beach. It's made of refreshingly rare gravel rather than sand, always remaining clean, dark, and wave washed. The conglomerate rock face rising above the beach is composed of 60-million-year-old sedimentary rocks. Worship the waves from nearby flat and smooth rock surfaces at neighboring Weston Beach, which is lined with colorful pebbles and scattered driftwood.

At 2.1 miles, reach The Slot, a narrow channel that absorbs the shock of big and persistent waves. The trail becomes Sand Hill Trail and you reach Sand Hill Cove, which is partially bordered by a 100-foot-tall sedimentary rock cliff face and sports a pebbly beach, an ideal spot for watching the foamy white water and the quiet harbor seals that resemble fat cigars. At a trail junction, go left for a short loop which overlooks Sea Lion Cove to the south and Headland

Sand Hill Cove, winter

Cove to the north. Note the stark contrast between the opening of Headland Cove, where the waves explode loudly against rock outcrops, and the serene Headland Cove beach, with its perfect soft and dark sand.

Retrace your steps to the junction and continue straight. After the trail nears and then heads away from the road, there is another junction. Continue straight to the Cypress Grove Trail at 3.2 miles. It makes a loop as it passes through coastal scrub including golden yarrow, sage, coyote brush, and monkeyflower while showing scenes of The Pinnacle punctuating wind-stunted Monterey cypresses. Head back toward the road, but turn left onto Whalers Knoll Trail just before reaching the road. Wind around and climb 200 feet to Whalers Knoll through an open Monterey pine forest.

Descend from this view-laden perch to a trail junction and turn left to reach beachless Bluefish Cove, which is semi-surrounded by steep and stark rock cliffs. Continue on Cabin Trail and come to Whalers Cabin at 4.8 miles. Note the huge and gnarled Monterey cypresses that shade the cabin—these trees are native almost exclusively to Point Lobos. The trail then splits through dense coyote brush, with views of calm and kelp-coated Whalers Cove and beyond to Granite Point.

Pass the Carmelo Meadow Trail on your right and go straight onto Granite Point Trail. From various vistas on this trail, you can gaze in all directions beyond granite and scrub to check out lengthy Carmel River State Beach, among other attractions. A maze of low-growing native succulents in the *Dudleya* genus, such as bluff lettuce, decorate the north-facing banks above a cove called The Pit.

Retrace your steps to the Carmelo Meadow Trail and return to your car amid a variety of herbs, grasses, and rushes.

57 ☙ BLACK MOUNTAIN AND STEVENS CREEK

Distance: 5.4-mile loop
Difficulty: Moderate to strenuous
High point: 2800 feet
Elevation gain: 1300 feet
Map: USGS Mindego Hill
Nearest campground: Sunol Campground, phone (510) 636-1684
Information: Midpeninsula Regional Open Space District, phone
  (650) 691-1200

For the entire midpeninsula, this hike rates among the best for views, trail variety, and diversity of native plants. It is in an open space preserve called Monte Bello, which is Italian for "beautiful mountain," and the many splendid vistas displaying fine rows of Santa Cruz Mountains fit the name. Climb rolling grasslands to 2800-foot-tall Black Mountain, which is pure white heaven when it occasionally gets a snow dusting in winter. Finish by walking along the riparian corridor of serene Stevens Creek, which is as pleasant and pretty as it gets. Most of the hike is dry, so bring plenty of your own water. You can extend this hike into a fine backpack trip into neighboring Upper Stevens Creek County Park, or arrange for a car to pick you up there. Note that mountain bikers are allowed on all trails except the Stevens Creek Trail.

From I-280 in Palo Alto, turn west onto paved Page Mill Road and travel 7.6 winding miles to the very large parking lot (it's signed) on the left.

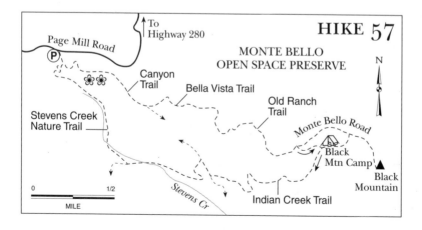

West view from Black Mountain, autumn

Walk 0.1 mile to a stone bench at a vista point and gaze at the source of Stevens Creek below, which follows the San Andreas Fault zone. The largest mountain far to the south, past tiers of densely clothed Santa Cruz Mountains, is Mount Umunhum, which is very close to the epicenter of the 1989 earthquake.

The connector trail to Canyon Trail (bear left) heads eastward along a grassy ridge where coyote brush takes hold. In late winter, look for blue-eyed grass poking through the greenery, followed in spring by another native wildflower, California poppy.

Turn right onto Canyon Trail at 0.3 mile, and promptly come to a cluster of canyon live oaks, featuring intertwining roots—it looks like one large, multitrunked oak. After passing a sag pond clogged with cattails and other native perennials, break away from the shade and bear left for a 400-foot climb over 0.8 mile on the Bella Vista ("beautiful view") Trail. True to its name, the trail offers long-distance scenery mainly to the south, including Black Mountain's northwest shoulder. This narrow trail eventually looks down into the canyon of Stevens Creek, with California bay laurel and oak woodland on the west facing slope and Douglas fir forest on the east facing slope.

Turn right onto signed Old Ranch Trail at 1.4 miles. The photogenic views are mainly to the west—dark gray rain clouds floating in from the ocean can create a mystical and ominous effect as they rise over the mostly evergreen mountains. A grove of statuesque buckeye trees at 1.8 miles can look dead but provocative by early autumn because their leaves have shriveled in natural response to drought.

Turn right at Black Mountain Camp (2.2 miles), make a note of the signed Indian Creek Trail (your return route), and then go left on an old dirt road for the final 200-foot climb to transmitter-topped Black Mountain. The actual high point is a grassy knoll, but your best views will feature a foreground of chaparral such as coyote brush, toyon, ceanothus, coffeeberry, and chamise. The idea here is to circle the large mountaintop and capture the numerous commanding vistas—San Jose and Diablo Valley to the east and the Pacific Ocean to the west.

At 2.8 miles, get on the dirt road known as Indian Creek Trail, which at first plunges down a steep canyonside laden with chamise and occasional licorice-scented fennel. Farther downslope, coyote brush is joined by coffeeberry and toyon with scattered buckeye groves. Then coast live oak, white oak, laurel, and sporadic madrone make appearances.

Turn right on the signed Canyon Trail at 4 miles, climb 0.2 mile, and then bear left onto the signed single-track trail called Stevens Creek Nature Trail. Self-guided with informative signs, this mostly shaded and sheltered nature trail contrasts noticeably with the previous trails, with Douglas fir, bay, and occasional bigleaf maple draping branches over the path. There's a feel of solitude and whisper-still intimacy tucked below the grassy and windswept slopes.

Cross modest and attractive Stevens Creek, bear right at a trail junction, and then climb 1 gradual mile to the parking lot. Watch for slow-moving California newts and fast-dashing western fence lizards at your feet.

58 ⚐ FRANCISCAN LOOP TRAIL

Distance: 3.3-mile loop
Difficulty: Easy
High point: 2100 feet
Elevation gain: 400 feet
Map: USGS Mindego Hill
Nearest campground: Sunol Campground, phone (510) 636-1684
Information: Midpeninsula Regional Open Space District, phone (650) 691-1200

Wander past open brushland and deep into cool forest in Los Trancos Open Space Preserve. It's a bonafide stomp in the wild woods, from where the gleaming skyscrapers edging San Francisco Bay can be admired on clear days. This hike also features a couple of odd and craggy limestone outcrops and a few tremendous bay trees that are equally peculiar. Don't forget to pick up a brochure at the trailhead and read the little numbered signposts along the way to learn about violent plate movements, grinding earth action, and what it's like being in the middle of the San Andreas Fault Zone. The preserve is an ideal spot to be unceremoniously caught in a winter downpour. In fact, winter's a good time to visit overall—the creeks are rising, the organic duff keeps the ground moist, and life is good. The creeks are not reliable sources of water in all seasons though, so bring your own.

From I-280 in Palo Alto, head west on paved Page Mill Road and travel 7.6 winding miles to the large parking lot on the right (Monte Bello Open Space Preserve trailheads are across the road).

This journey begins in a clockwise direction with the signed Franciscan Loop Trail and finishes with the self-guided San Andreas Fault Trail. Commence from a gap at the parking lot. Take either trail (one allows cyclists) and stay on the Franciscan Loop Trail, walking briefly through a unique mix of chaparral that consists mainly of coyote brush with occasional coffeeberry and fern. A descent promptly ensues into a hardwood forest of black oak, canyon live oak, bay laurel, and madrone.

Pass a trail leading right (your return route), and soon cross slender Los Trancos Creek followed by a couple of tall bigleaf maple trees

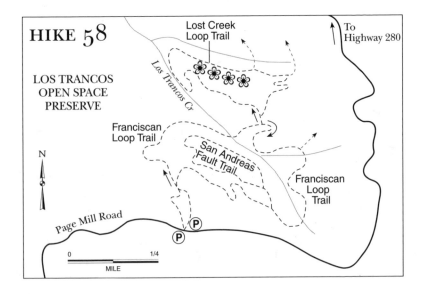

Franciscan Loop Trail

and a signed trail junction with the Lost Creek Loop Trail. Bear left, walk the loop clockwise, and at 0.9 mile, reunite with the creek. Wind east then follow close to well-shaded Lost Creek, which is bordered by currant (flowers in early spring), false Solomon's seal, trillium, wood fern, and star flower. Complete this short loop and turn left to regain the Franciscan Loop Trail, where ocean spray, blackberry, and hazelnut bushes join a lush understory of ferns and spring-flowering western azalea.

After passing a pair of impressively sized rock outcrops, climb briefly to a signed junction at 2 miles that points toward the San Andreas Fault Trail. Turn right and immediately walk through a large patch of fragrant native mugwort herbs. Then follow a seasonal stream. The bobcats in this area use gulches like these to prowl and get water. Look for the gargantuan, moss-covered bay laurel stump at trailside—nine grayish trunks have sprouted from the decayed stump to form a large laurel again.

Just before reaching the signed San Andreas Fault Trail, duck under a huge bay laurel branch leaning horizontally, then diagonally from its larger parent trunk. Walk the miniloop to learn about this area's earthquake history. Then rejoin the Franciscan Loop Trail, turn right and return to the trailhead. Before getting in your car, cross Page Mill Road and go l00 yards onto the signed Stevens Creek Nature Trail to capture a sprawling view southeastward of Black Mountain and Loma Prieta Mountain, the epicenter of the 1989 earthquake.

59 ❦ WINDY HILL AND HAMMS GULCH TRAIL

Distance: 9.6-mile loop
Difficulty: Moderate
High point: 1900 feet
Elevation gain: 1400 feet
Map: USGS Mindego Hill
Nearest campground: Portola State Park, phone (650) 948-9098
Information: Midpeninsula Regional Open Space District, phone
   (650) 691-1200

Grassy Windy Hill in the Windy Hill Open Space Preserve is a major
landmark in San Mateo County, known for its remarkable panorama
of the San Francisco Bay, the ocean, and the Santa Cruz Mountains.
Often breezy in the spring, it's sometimes dusted with snow in the
winter, a special time to visit. Autumn tends to have the best weather
for snagging views.

   This ambitious clockwise loop trip at first makes an easy climb up
Windy Hill, which can be seen from many spots on the peninsula. It

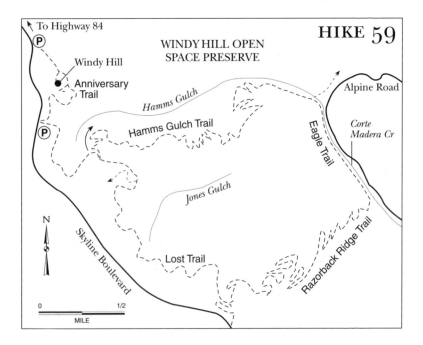

then proceeds down a gorgeously forested ridge to a valley floor and finally leads back up an equally impressive wooded ridge. The bulk of this hike is shaded, with the middle part wandering a ways up Corte Madera Creek. Be sure to bring plenty of your own water and note that you may encounter horses along the way.

From the junction of Highways 35 and 84 south of Palo Alto, drive south on 35 (also called Skyline Boulevard) for 2 miles. Park on the east side of the road in a small lot signed for Windy Hill.

Anniversary Trail, a hard-packed, yard-wide dirt path, climbs 100 feet in elevation through coyote brush, featuring extraordinary and seldom seen views of San Francisco Bay, the East Bay communities, and the Hayward Hills to the east. Short spur trails lead to two of the grassy knobs of Windy Hill, which is a popular kite flying and hang gliding spot.

Continue down and southward past coyote brush and another parking lot. The trail then stays flat past occasional stinging nettle and poison oak, with the previously mentioned eastward views gracing the scene all the way to the signed Hamms Gulch Trail at 1 mile, where you turn left.

Hamms Gulch Trail is a slender footpath of constant switchbacks down a tranquil ridge. Look for a few massive Douglas firs with extra wide trunks near this trail's start—some feature aboveground roots resembling a monstrous spider. The trail then rambles through a mature hardwood forest of tan oak, California bay laurel, and madrone trees. Some 2.5 miles down this trail, you pass next to Hamms Gulch, cross a bridge over Jones Gulch, and then veer right onto Eagle Trail.

This mostly flat trail stays happily near Corte Madera Creek for a country half mile and then reaches Razorback Ridge Trail at 4.4 miles. Unless you're as fit as a Tibetan Sherpa guide, you'll be huffing, puffing, and trudging up this 2.3-mile-long trail as it zigzags into small ravines and over ridge shoulders. Take your time to marvel at the tall oaks and madrones and to check out the views down the canyon. Before you know it, you're heading right onto Lost Trail at 6.6 miles.

This slender and mostly flat dirt path snakes gracefully just below another ridge top. The first half wanders through a mixed Douglas fir and hardwood forest with the scent of California bay laurel trees (some reaching 70 feet tall) filling your nostrils. The northern half of the trail breaks into shrubbery of mainly coyote brush, but also ocean spray, coffeeberry, blackberry, thimbleberry, cow parsnips, and poison oak. At 8.3 miles, pass Hamms Gulch Trail on your right. Continue straight to pass by Windy Hill again on the way to your car.

60 ⚘ GOLDEN CASCADE TO WADDELL BEACH

Distance: 17 miles one-way; 10.8 miles round trip to Silver Falls
Difficulty: Moderate
High point: 1500 feet
Elevation gain: 300 feet to Waddell Beach; 3100 feet round trip
Maps: USGS Big Basin, Franklin Point, Davenport, Año Nuevo
Nearest campground: Butano State Park, phone (650) 879-2040
Information: Big Basin Redwoods State Park, phone (408) 429-2851
   or (408) 338-6132

This journey is so jam-packed with scenic highlights and ecosystem variety that about the only California land features you won't see are alpine mountains and desert. Start amid giant redwoods where the grizzly bear once roamed. Then check out the distant ocean from patchworks of chaparral where the western fence lizard does push-ups and the ground squirrel scurries. Next on the visual attractions agenda is a series of cascades that seem to glide forever, followed by a pair of mighty waterfalls so breathtaking you'll be glad you brought extra film. The hike then plunges into a mixed evergreen forest that alternates with chaparral and eventually leads to a hardwood forest before following the classic Skyline to the Sea Trail. Refreshingly clear Waddell Creek flows by a verdant meadow to a marsh that serves as a sanctuary for up to 150 bird species before leading you to Waddell Beach.

This is the ideal off-season hike because summer tends to be foggy here, with ten times the people, while clear fall days allow for clear views. Late winter and spring are the best times to visit, for the falls and cascades are bigger, faster, and louder. It's best to take extra time to absorb this smorgasbord of visual charms by backpacking one-way down to Waddell Beach. Arrange for a car to pick you up there or take a Santa Cruz Metropolitan Transit District bus (408/425-8600) back to your starting point.

From the town of Boulder Creek (13 miles northwest of Santa Cruz on Highway 9), drive 9 miles northwest on Highway 236 to Big Basin Redwoods State Park Headquarters. From the north, drive Highway 236 8.4 miles from its junction with Highway 9.

Leave the parking lot and go right onto Sunset Trail. The trail at first traipses along tranquil Opal Creek beneath a canopy of massive

View from Windy Hill, autumn (Photo by Eric Soares)

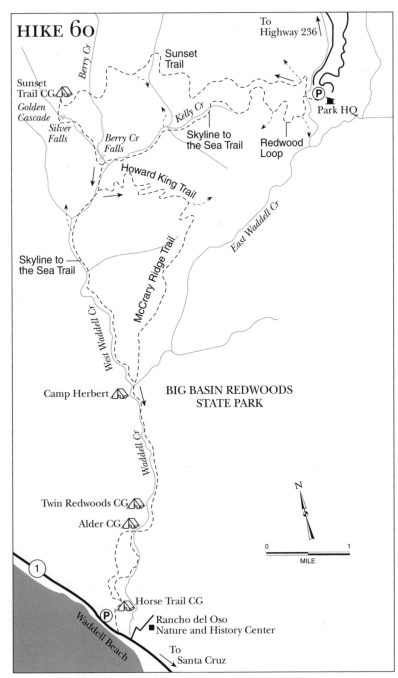

HIKE 60

To Highway 236

Berry Cr

Sunset Trail

Sunset Trail CG

Golden Cascade

Silver Falls

Berry Cr Falls

Kelly Cr

Skyline to the Sea Trail

Park HQ

Redwood Loop

Howard King Trail

McCrary Ridge Trail

East Waddell Cr

Skyline to the Sea Trail

West Waddell Cr

Camp Herbert

BIG BASIN REDWOODS STATE PARK

Waddell Cr

N

Twin Redwoods CG

Alder CG

0   1
MILE

1

Horse Trail CG

Waddell Beach

Rancho del Oso Nature and History Center

To Santa Cruz

redwoods that gradually shrink in size and number. After about 1 mile, a serious descent ensues, crossing two canyonsides in a mixed forest before alternating through forest and chaparral of manzanita, chamise, ceanothus, and knobcone pines. In 5.5 miles, a spur trail at a signed trail junction leads to Sunset Trail Camp, the park's most remote camp. Spend your first night here if backpacking.

Golden Cascade slides and plummets a short distance from the camp. Flanked by rugged and rusty rocky walls embedded with soft green mosses and ferns, wonderful Golden Cascade can be followed and studied for a good 0.25 mile. At the bottom there's a splendid view down on Silver Falls, which plunge some 60 vertical feet straight down past a toppled redwood trunk that leans 15 feet above an oblong pool of clear water. Descend 0.5 mile and reach a vista that overlooks Berry Creek Falls. They pour and splash over dark and slippery rock walls some 70 feet into a small, sand-bottomed pool. Stop at the observation deck at 6.8 miles, about halfway down the falls, to sniff the cool mist.

Just beyond Berry Creek Falls, reach a trail junction and turn right. Follow Skyline to the Sea Trail briefly, and then bear left onto Howard King Trail, which climbs gently for 2.5 miles in a shady mixed evergreen forest of bay laurel, madrone, and Douglas fir. Watch for the shrub-concealed sign for McCrary Ridge Trail at 9.8 miles. Go right and descend past chaparral of knobcone pine and manzanita that foregrounds views of the Waddell Creek Canyon sprawling to the sea. You soon plunge back into a mixed evergreen forest and eventually turn left back onto Skyline to the Sea Trail at 13.2 miles. Cross a bridge over East Waddell Creek and reach Camp Herbert. Consider spending a second night here if backpacking.

Berry Creek Falls, late spring

The rest of the hike follows the course of Waddell Creek, past flourishing bigleaf maple, alder, buckeye, bay laurel, redwood, and Douglas fir, with an understory of fern, thimbleberry, horsetail, and redwood sorrel. Binoculars come in handy at the large and undisturbed freshwater marsh at 16.5 miles, which is home to scores of ducks and herons.

61 ⚡ MONTARA MOUNTAIN AND BROOKS CREEK FALLS

Distance: 7.2 miles round trip; 2.8-mile loop to Brooks Creek Falls view
Difficulty: Strenuous
High point: 1900 feet
Elevation gain: 2300 feet
Map: USGS Montara Mountain
Nearest campground: Azalea Flat Winter Camp, phone (650) 363-4021 or (650) 948-9098
Information: San Pedro Valley Park, phone (650) 355-8289

Until this book came out, Brooks Creek Falls was either a mysterious secret or a treat innocently gone unnoticed. If it's January through March and you're driving through Pacifica with a couple of hours to kill, Brooks Creek Falls are a perfect stop. They make a great photo using a telephoto lens, virtually without shade almost all day long.

The trick to enjoying this three-tiered, 175-foot-long cataract is to visit during late winter and early spring, especially after a spell of rain. Chances are Brooks Creek Falls have shriveled to nonexistence during other times. If you're in the mood for fabulous views, choose a clear day (autumn is the most likely time) and consider arranging for a second car at Montara Beach. This allows you to climb Montara Mountain and then descend 3 miles along the Old San Pedro Road Trail with sea and beach views greeting you the whole way.

From south Pacifica on Highway 1, turn east onto Linda Mar Boulevard and drive 2 miles to signed San Pedro Valley Park.

Signed Brooks Creek Trail climbs all the way, first in a Douglas fir forest and then through a tall eucalyptus grove. The trail soon overlooks the steep banks of coastal scrub on the far side of seasonal Brooks Creek, a tributary to San Pedro Creek. A magnificent display of native chaparral shrubs now decorates the trail. At first coffeeberry, ocean spray, and three kinds of manzanita dominate. Farther on, toyon and coyote brush enter the scene, with evergreen huckleberry and occasional coast silktassel occupying the semi-shaded spots while Pacific wax myrtle shows up in seepage areas.

A bench at 0.7 mile reveals the first sighting of Brooks Creek Falls across the open canyon. There's an equally commanding view here of Sweeney Ridge, from which Spanish explorer Captain Gaspar de Portola first saw San Francisco Bay. Long and skinny, Brooks Creek Falls topples and streams over an intensely steep coastal scrub cliff with little resemblance to typical waterfalls. As you leave this manzanita-surrounded

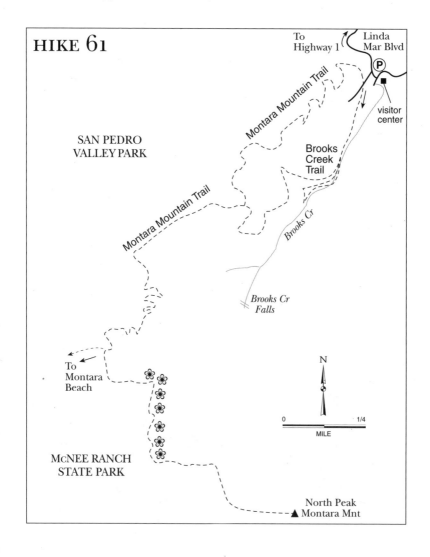

HIKE 61

To Highway 1 / Linda Mar Blvd

Montara Mountain Trail

P

visitor center

SAN PEDRO VALLEY PARK

Brooks Creek Trail

Montara Mountain Trail

Brooks Cr

Brooks Cr Falls

To Montara Beach

N

McNEE RANCH STATE PARK

0 — 1/4
MILE

North Peak
▲ Montara Mnt

bench, admire a handsome trio of shrub-form madrones neighbored by a scattering of Monterey pines punctuating the eroded slope.

Continue on the trail and look for a final side view of Brooks Creek Falls at 1.1 miles, next to an unusually huge manzanita that you could barely wrap your arms around—the tree leans sideways over the trail. Three hundred yards farther, the trail climbs to a ridge top and T-junction featuring a view that encompasses Linda Mar Beach and Pacifica. The journey continues left and up along the Montara Mountain Trail (the return route is to the right).

When the trail soon becomes a dirt road, go left to reach Montara Mountain (Montara Beach is 3 miles to the right). At 2.2 miles, heavy-duty climbing begins, eased in spring by pretty lupine and California poppy. Blue blossom ceanothus (flowers in May) begin dominating the chaparral slopes at 2.5 miles, with views of nearby rock outcrops of granite from the Salinian block. Other boulder outcrops you'll admire here consist of shale, conglomerate, and sandstone.

Stray off the beaten path a couple of times to scale your choice of small rock-and-grass knobs that appear from 3 to 3.3 miles. Soon after, you reach Montara Mountain proper, which is part of the Santa Cruz Mountains. Red-tailed hawks and peregrine falcons soar over this grassy, boulder-strewn mountain while coyotes, mountain lions, and gray foxes hide in the Montara manzanita (which only grows here) and ceanothus scrub.

Pacifica from Montara Mountain Trail, early winter

62 ❦ MOUNT LIVERMORE AND ANGEL ISLAND

Distance: 7-mile loop
Difficulty: Moderate
High point: 781 feet
Elevation gain: 800 feet
Map: USGS San Francisco North
Nearest campground: China Camp State Park, phone (415) 456-0766
Information: Angel Island State Park, phone (415) 456-1286 or
    (415) 435-1915

Standing atop Mount Livermore is like being a special angel hovering
high above the virtual center of San Francisco Bay. Dramatic scenery
abounds in all directions, and even snapshots on clear days become
photographic masterpieces. Named after Marin County conservation-
ist Caroline Livermore, Mount Livermore rises majestically to crown

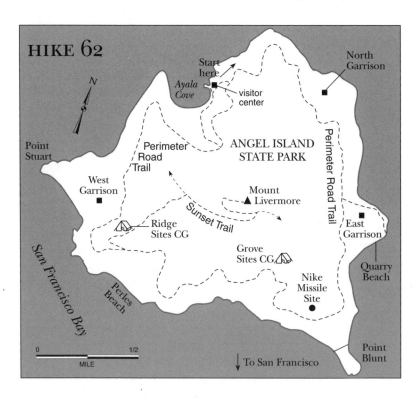

circle-shaped and fittingly named Angel Island. Backpackers often choose a full moon to scurry up steep Sunset Trail at night to marvel at the blurry city lights and shiny gray bay from the flat crest of this rounded mountain. Moonless nights on Mount Livermore are also a treat, when the lights of Golden Gate Bridge and San Francisco twinkle and sparkle like a magic wand.

As you ferry over to Angel Island, the Bay Area's most prominent and biggest island, imagine yourself in a long and swift tule boat built thousands of years ago by the Miwok Indians. They were expert fishermen who also gathered acorns and hunted ducks, deer, and seals from Angel Island. When you disembark at Ayala Cove, harken back to 1775, when Spain's Juan Manuel de Ayala anchored here to record the first known maps of the bay. Some 130 years later, North Garrison was converted to a controversial Immigration Station, where mostly Asians were processed in sometimes inhumane fashion.

Shorebirds including blue herons and pelicans visit the multiple-cove island while sparrows, scrub jays, robins, hummingbirds, owls, hawks, and flickers hang out indefinitely. It's a mystery how raccoons and deer inhabit the island while other Marin woodland animals such as skunks, squirrels, coyotes, and foxes, are notably absent.

Visit in autumn to escape summer fog and to obtain the clearest views. You'll encounter fewer people in winter, but note that ferries from Tiburon run only on weekends during winter months. At other times of the year, ferries depart daily (call 415/435-2131 for a schedule of sailing times). Ferries also leave from San Francisco and Vallejo (call 1-800-BAY-CRUISE). Backpackers must make reservations year-round (call 1-800-444-7275).

From Marin City on Highway 1, drive US 101 north to Tiburon Boulevard (also known as Highway 131) and turn east. After 4 miles, park at a pay lot, and then walk briefly to the Tiburon ferry.

Northridge Trail begins with a steep ascent past stalky and juvenile coast live oak (Angel Island natives) and windswept Monterey pines (native to Point Lobos). Gaze past native toyon to observe the sailboats cruising the bay.

Reach the mostly paved Perimeter Road Trail at 0.3 mile and go left. The trail stays mostly flat and reaches fully landscaped North Garrison at 1.2 miles, where tall cedars and eucalyptus trees tower. A bit farther, check out the three-story-high hospital where U.S. military men were treated for lingering tropical diseases. A side trail leads to wind-protected Quarry Beach. East Garrison comes next on this clockwise tour at 2.2 miles. These mess halls and barracks

Tiburon Peninsula from Angel Island, winter

housed some 30,000 military men per year destined for overseas duty.

Continue around to the south side of Angel Island, where immense eucalyptus stands have been cleared to aid in the return of native chaparral (toyon, chamise, coyote brush, and manzanita) and native trees (oaks and madrones). As these plants establish themselves, the cleared area allows for gorgeous wide-open views of Alcatraz and San Francisco.

At 4 miles, Sunset Trail takes off to the right from a vantage point overlooking windy Perles Beach. The route ascends unmercifully 500 feet in elevation past coastal scrub and chaparral to 781-foot-tall Mount Livermore. Dome-shaped Mount Livermore now offers picnic tables instead of antiaircraft guns that once were fixtures here.

Retrace your steps and continue north on Perimeter Road Trail, soon entering a shady grove of mature pines, oaks, and cypresses overlooking the chapel and stables of West Garrison. Turn left at a trail junction above Ayala Cove to return to the ferry landing.

63 ⚘ SAN PABLO RIDGE

Distance: 11.5-mile loop
Difficulty: Moderate
High point: 1250 feet
Elevation gain: 1500 feet
Map: USGS Richmond
Nearest campground: Bort Meadow Campground, phone (510) 635-0135
Information: East Bay Regional Park District, phone (510) 635-0135

Thankfully isolated Wildcat Canyon Regional Park is a well-kept secret, tucked cozily away in the Berkeley foothills. The views of San Pablo Reservoir and San Francisco Bay from San Pablo Ridge and Wildcat Peak are unsurpassed. For maximum enjoyment, visit on a day with high visibility (autumn is the most likely time). The gently sculpted hills are a cheerful green in spring, dotted with wildflowers and alive with chirping birds fluttering in the oaks scattered across the open landscape. Bring plenty of your own water and note that mountain bikers and horses also use trails along this hike.

From I-80 southbound in Richmond, take the McBryde Avenue exit and go east on this road until it dead-ends at the trailhead. If travelling northbound on I-80, take the Amador/Solano exit to McBryde Avenue.

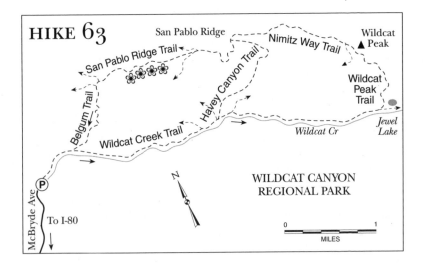

San Pablo Reservoir from Wildcat Peak, winter

To start, get on Wildcat Creek Trail, which promptly climbs on an old, run-down paved road (no vehicles allowed). Note the return route on the left at 0.5 mile and continue following above the meandering course of lovely Wildcat Creek. Sprawling Wildcat Canyon appears on the right at 0.9 mile, with ancient coast live oak and bay laurel coating the slopes.

The inaugural merger with willow- and alder-lined Wildcat Creek occurs near a eucalyptus-bordered wooden bridge at 2.1 miles. Continue straight at a three-way trail junction and then climb a few yards farther (cut your trip in half here by going left onto Havey Canyon Trail, named after a dairy farmer who raised Spanish longhorn cattle). The path stays mostly flat along the ensuing 2 miles, past a sequence of gullies clogged with blackberry bushes and willows; all of them channel water swiftly into Wildcat Creek in late winter and early spring.

Just before reaching Jewel Lake (a duck pond), go left onto unsigned Wildcat Peak Trail (a dirt path) next to two signposts at 4.1 miles. Climb through eucalyptus and then chaparral, following the signs to the peak at all junctions. Heavy breathing ceases atop 1250-foot-high Wildcat Peak at 5.6 miles, and gasping begins with a spectacular panorama. Angel Island and the Golden Gate Bridge adorn San Francisco Bay, which is guarded by Mount Tamalpais to the west. Mount Diablo rises in the distance over San Pablo Reservoir to the east.

Descend the peak's east face via any of several footpaths, then head north at the trail junction onto Nimitz Way Trail. Crooked-trunked Monterey pines and squat coyote brush are scattered over the grasslands along this ridgetop path, which promptly converts from broken asphalt to an old dirt road. Pass a corral at 8.5 miles, head left, and then go right 100 yards farther onto signed San Pablo Ridge Trail. Enjoy another 1.5 miles worth of far-reaching Berkeley foothill and bay views while climbing a handful of knolls.

Go left onto Belgum Trail at 10 miles, and be sure to look back to admire lovely San Pablo Ridge. The views of the bay vanish as you descend 700 feet in elevation past cactus, palms, and eucalyptus to eventually reunite with signed Wildcat Creek Trail at 10.9 miles. Go right to return to the trailhead.

64 ⚘ WEBB AND REDWOOD CREEKS

Distance: 13 miles round trip; 6.8 miles round trip to Pantoll
  Ranger Station
Difficulty: Moderate to strenuous
High point: 1500 feet
Elevation gain: 2700 feet
Maps: USGS San Rafael, Bolinas
Nearest campground: Mount Tamalpais State Park, phone (415)
  388-2070
Information: Mount Tamalpais State Park, phone (415) 388-2070

Several splendid creeks drain off the slopes of Mount Tamalpais, but Webb and Redwood Creeks are arguably the most spectacular. The coastal Miwok Indians, who thrived in this area for thousands of years, gave the gradually uplifting mountain its name, which is Spanish for "the country of the Tamal Indians."

This excursion explores some 6 miles of cascades, miniwaterfalls, and rapids that these two creeks feature from midwinter until late spring. The rest of the year these creeks are calmer but still crystal clear and generously bordered by cathedral-like redwoods. The journey opens with tremendous views of colorful and renowned Stinson Beach as you climb through coastal scrub and grassland adorned with wildflowers in spring. Cozy and scenic Van Wyck Meadow is a prime picnic spot farther along. Then you follow Redwood Creek downstream to the world's largest cluster of mammoth redwoods in Muir

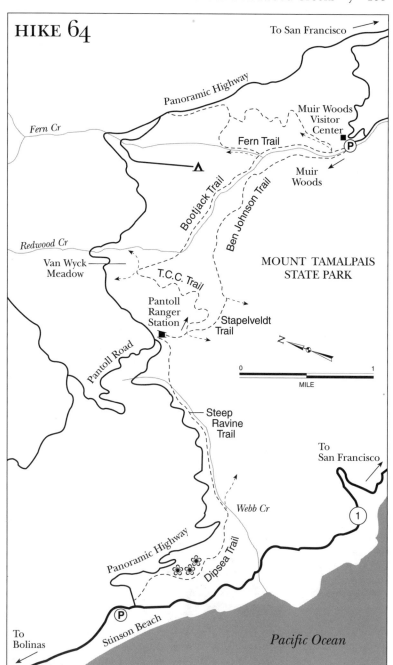

HIKE 64

To San Francisco

Panoramic Highway

Fern Cr

Muir Woods
Visitor
Center
Ⓟ

Fern Trail

Muir
Woods

Bootjack Trail

Ben Johnson Trail

Redwood Cr

Van Wyck
Meadow

T.C.C. Trail

MOUNT TAMALPAIS
STATE PARK

Pantoll
Ranger
Station

Stapelveldt
Trail

N

Pantoll Road

0   1
MILE

Steep
Ravine
Trail

To
San Francisco

Webb Cr

①

Panoramic Highway

Dipsea Trail

Ⓟ

To
Bolinas

Stinson Beach

Pacific Ocean

Woods. Arrange for a car to meet you here and cut the hike in half.

From US 101 north of San Francisco, take the Stinson Beach exit (Highway 1). A few seconds before parking at Stinson Beach, note the signed Dipsea Trail where Panoramic Highway meets Highway 1 (also called Shoreline Highway). To reach Muir Woods, drive the Panoramic Highway from Highway 1 to a lower road signed for Muir Woods. It's 1.5 miles on this paved road to the parking lot.

Dipsea Trail (home of a legendary foot race) and Steep Ravine Trail take you two-thirds the way up Mount Tamalpais. From the get-go, climb in shaded woods. Then break into coastal scrub featuring orange bush monkeyflower and lizard's tail shrubs. Dipsea Trail then cuts through sloping grassland blanketed with greenery and highlighted by poppies, blue-eyed grass, and lupines in the spring. Catch your breath during the climb by stopping to take in sweeping views of Stinson Beach, with its gracefully rolling surf and long, wide sand strip.

At 1.3 miles, meet wondrous Webb Creek and head left onto Steep Ravine Trail. Five wooden bridges take you across this shaded stream, which charges wildly in spots, cascading over huge boulders. Duck under several toppled redwood archways and eventually climb a 15-rung ladder. Giant redwoods continue to dominate the forest bordering the creek, shading profuse thimbleberry and sword fern.

Continue climbing to Pantoll Ranger Station at 3.4 miles. Head south to connect with Stapelveldt and T.C.C. Trails. Bear left onto the latter. This trail was built during World War I by the Tamalpais Conservation Corps, and offers teasing glimpses of Mount Tamalpais' crest beyond Douglas fir limbs as it stays level and shaded across a series of tranquil ravines.

Stinson Beach at low tide, winter

After 1 mile, reach a clearing (Van Wyck Meadow) dominated by a huge boulder in the middle that invites a climb. This flat field is surrounded by lush coast live oaks, Douglas firs, and bay laurels. Go right onto Bootjack Trail and meet a boulder-filled section of glorious Redwood Creek after 0.5 mile of downhill tread. Then plunge steeply into a deep and cool Douglas fir forest adorned with ferns and bigleaf maples. Cross a large wooden bridge and then concentrate on the steady and comforting tumble of Redwood Creek as you reunite with sheltering redwoods.

After 1.8 miles on the Bootjack Trail, continue straight onto Fern Trail at a trail junction at 6.2 miles. Note the signposts depicting the legacy of these primeval and noble redwoods and some nearby Douglas fir giants, such as the 273-foot-tall William Kent Memorial. Reach the Muir Woods Visitor Center in another mile and sip from the fountain.

For the return trip, take the level Hillside Trail that leads to the ascending Ben Johnson Trail. Both trails allow you to look down on a sea of massive redwoods. Turn right onto Stapelveldt Trail and soon reach the Pantoll Ranger Station. Listen for the raunchy squawk of a Steller's jay as you return along these trails, and if it's near dusk, listen for the barking call of a spotted owl.

65 ⚘ MOUNT TAMALPAIS SUMMIT VIA CATARACT FALLS

Distance: 13 miles round trip; 6.5 miles one-way to East Peak
Difficulty: Moderate to strenuous
High point: 2571 feet
Elevation gain: 2300 feet
Maps: USGS San Rafael, Bolinas
Nearest campground: Mount Tamalpais State Park, phone (415) 388-2070
Information: Marin Municipal Water District, phone (415) 924-4600 or (415) 459-5267

Find out firsthand why so many poets have expressed the virtues of magical Mount Tamalpais, by taking the ultimate route to its tippy top (East Peak). This trip offers intimacy with Mount Tam's largest lake (Alpine Lake) and then climbs in a mixed forest to a series of cascades (Cataract Falls) that charge down a rocky and wooded canyon. Comprised of a mix of open grassland, steep canyons, and hardwood forests, Mount Tamalpais is home to an impressive twelve species of oaks, including hybrids. You'll pass by several of these along this varied

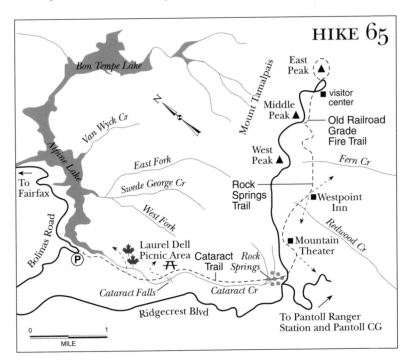

HIKE 65

walk in wild woods. Farther on, visit a famous outdoor theater and a historic old inn before gawking at unsurpassed views of San Francisco Bay and San Pablo Bay from atop East Peak. These romantic views are most likely to be the clearest in autumn, and since paved Ridgecrest Boulevard climbs to nearly the top of East Peak, you can arrange for a car to meet you and cut the hike in half.

Drive Sir Francis Drake Highway to Fairfax, northwest of San Rafael. Turn southeast on Claus Drive, followed by an immediate left onto Broadway, and then an immediate right onto paved Bolinas Road. After 8.2 curving miles, cross Alpine Lake's dam and park on the side of the road at the hairpin turn.

Signed Cataract Trail begins a slight climb, with views down on a slender and attractive arm of Alpine Lake, elevation 644 feet. The well-built trail is comfortably shaded courtesy of a hardwood and mixed conifer forest of tan oak, redwood, bigleaf maple, and hazelnut. The 750-foot elevation gain to Cataract Falls intensifies near a trail junction at 0.6 mile, where profuse ferns and thickets of huckleberry shrubs join the dense and soothing woods.

Continue straight, and 0.5 mile farther, the roar of the falls intensifies as the canyon steepens. The giant live oaks are so sheltered here that their trunks are draped with tiny ferns and mosses, enhancing this mystic fairytale setting. A dinky side trail brings you up close to the falls, which spill, slide, and plunge over slippery smooth boulders into clusters of puddles and pools in autumn. Come spring, the rains that wash down the ravines transform Cataract Falls into streaming white rapids, foam, and spray that drown out a human yell.

Another ideal hangout place is nearby Laurel Dell Picnic Area at 1.5 miles. Its large clearing is surrounded by ruggedly good-looking bay laurel, live oak, bigleaf maple, and Douglas fir. From here, continue an easy climb near the shaded banks of Cataract Creek for 1.3 miles to Rock Springs. Cross Ridgecrest Boulevard and follow the trail and signs east then north to Mountain Theater, which features 3,500 rock seats used for weddings and outdoor plays.

Spend the next 0.5 mile in dense shade on the Rock Springs Trail, crossing three bridges bordered by ferns and bay laurel. At 4.5 miles into the hike, reach Westpoint Inn, nestled in the forest and framed by the Golden Gate Bridge and Angel Island. Check out this stately stone lodge, which provides welcome shelter during a winter rain storm. Find the signed Old Railroad Grade Fire Road Trail near this architecturally significant but long-deserted structure and resume climbing.

Mount Tamalpais Summit, late winter

Orange bush monkeyflower adorns the trailside now, and there are views eastward of San Pablo Bay and Mount Diablo in the distance. Pause at a sign noting Westpoint Inn where a grand Douglas fir foregrounds Alcatraz Island, the Bay Bridge, and towering skyscrapers. The old dirt road stays mostly level all the way to the visitor center, with dense chaparral blocking the north winds. Several oak types, some Douglas fir, and yerba santa shrubs compliment the sweeping vistas now westward to the ocean. Reach the summit parking lot and then climb 400 feet in elevation along the rocky trail to East Peak.

From atop the numerous boulder clusters, you can gaze south and west to admire the ocean. Check out the sailboats cruising San Francisco Bay to the south and east. Photogenic Mount Diablo dominates to the east, rising over San Pablo Bay and the Richmond Bridge. The chaotic jumble topping East Peak was slowly created when the westward-moving North American plate clashed with the eastward-moving Farallon plate. Most of the rocks here consist of serpentine, sandstone, radiolarian chert, and quartz.

66 § COASTAL TRAIL AND HAYPRESS CAMP

Distance: 10.8 miles round trip to Haypress Camp; 5.5 miles one-way to Rodeo Beach
Difficulty: Moderate to strenuous
High point: 700 feet
Elevation gain: 2600 feet one-way
Map: USGS Point Bonita
Nearest campground: China Camp State Park, phone (415) 456-0766
Information: Golden Gate National Recreation Area, phone (415) 556-0560 or (415) 331-1540

This journey scales numerous grassy hills, and rest assured there's a grand vista from atop each one, revealing cute coves and secret, unnamed beaches. The trade off is that your legs will burn like a locomotive and your breath will be taken away by all the exerting climbs and the rewarding views each hilltop presents.

The hike originates from scenic Muir Beach, one of the most popular beaches in the Bay Area, and winds up at another classic placename, Rodeo Beach. In between, powerful surf pounds Tennessee Beach. Backpackers can veer off the main trail to reach Haypress Camp (call 415/331-1540 to make a required reservation). Day hikers continue to Rodeo Beach, where a waiting second car will keep you from

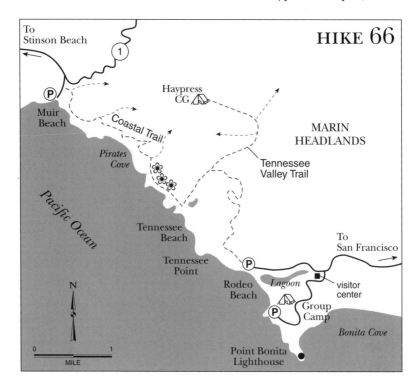

facing the sometimes pesky north winds on the return trip. You're most likely to get the best views in autumn, and the most solitude in winter.

Drive from San Francisco across the Golden Gate Bridge on US 101. Take the Highway 1 exit and then turn left onto Shoreline Highway (still Highway 1). Follow it west to signed Muir Beach and its huge parking lot. To reach Rodeo Beach, drive US 101 from San Francisco and take the Alexander Avenue exit. Follow all signs indicating the Marin Headlands, following Conzelman, McCullough, and then Bunker Roads.

The Coastal Trail leads to a knoll at 0.3 mile, with a picture-perfect view behind you of Muir Beach and its neighboring pastures. Mount Tamalpais looms in the distance. A half mile farther, reach a trail junction and stay to the right. There's an ideal view south and down into the rocky surf of Pirates Cove. Green Gulch and Coyote Ridge to the east complete the scene. They are ablaze in gold when the annual grasses dry in autumn, and become a blanket of cheery green during the winter rainy season.

The Coastal Trail now switches from old dirt road to well-graded footpath and heads past a virtually undisturbed coastal scrub mosaic of coyote brush, orange bush monkeyflower, and bush lupine (blue flowers in spring). A spur trail follows a seasonal stream to secluded Pirates Cove and its tiny sandy beach, a beautiful spot to take photos and reenergize yourself. A tenacious climb ensues, gaining 600 feet in elevation in 0.6 mile. Reach a trail junction on a flat at 2.3 miles.

Just when you're thinking "it doesn't get any better than this," it does. The slim footpath stays precariously yet refreshingly close to the extremely steep cliff tops, with each precious step rendering a top-of-the-world feeling. Lovely San Francisco provides a backdrop to Tennessee Beach and its neighboring stark and rocky cliffs. In all, there are four miniature capes to explore here, the final pair revealing intimate scenes of the gracefully curving Tennessee Valley and its lagoon, which is usually loaded with ducks and herons.

Descend steeply past some poison oak, with views down on a clandestine, cocoa brown beach, and then reach Tennessee Beach at 3.4 miles. It's a great spot for a picnic, and to reflect back to a foggy night in 1853 when the steamship Tennessee was abandoned with 600 passengers aboard. It then ran aground here, and the thundering wave action blasted the ship to pieces.

Proceed inland along the bottom of a broad U-shaped valley, past a lagoon encased in lupine and cow parsnip. Continue climbing gently on the wide gravel path (Tennessee Valley Trail) past mustard and poppy (both flowering in the spring). If backpacking, head left at a trail junction at 4.8 miles, follow a small stream, and reach Haypress Camp at 5.4 miles.

The ridge top is only 0.7 mile farther along the main trail, but it's the sweatiest and lung-screechingest climb of the trip. The rewards include a handful of bunkers built during World War II and a cluster of wind-stunted conifers. Toward the top, an amazing panorama begins to unfold, revealing this journey's most far-reaching views. Gaze at Tennessee Valley and Beach, Mount Tamalpais, the gray blue sea, Golden Gate Bridge, and Rodeo Beach and its pretty lagoon.

Muir Beach, winter

67 🌿 COAST TRAIL TO ALAMERE FALLS

Distance: 15.5 miles one-way; 6.6 miles round trip to Sculptured Beach
Difficulty: Moderate
High point: 600 feet
Elevation gain: 1900 feet one-way
Maps: USGS Drakes Bay, Inverness, Double Point
Nearest campground: Samuel P. Taylor State Park, phone (415) 488-9897
Information: Point Reyes National Seashore, phone (415) 663-1092

When Sir Frances Drake landed his ship here, he must have envied the Miwok Indians he hung out with. They roamed a shoreline that featured expansive, changing, stunning vistas of chalky white cliffs, sweeping hills, and pristine beaches. This epic journey includes all that and is also a birdwatcher's paradise, exploring several creeks, three ponds, and four freshwater lakes along an isolated and gorgeous stretch of Point Reyes National Seashore. Combining freshwater with saltwater and riparian zones allows plenty of chances to admire many of the 361 known bird species that fly over these U-shaped valleys and rugged bluffs.

Your destination is spectacular Alamere Falls. Well, actually, the falls are rather mediocre in summer and fall, but in late winter and early spring, they're a turbo-charged blast of white spray and jets that tumble out of control to a beach. In autumn, when the creeks are tiny and the days and views are usually the nicest, the hills are sheets of golden brown. But soon after the rains arrive, these sprawling hills are awash in green from the new annual grasses.

This route selection is designed to keep the pesky north winds at your back, in the hope there's a car waiting for you at journey's end. If you want more time to explore Point Reyes' wonders, consider staying a night or two at one of the backpacking camps. Note that you may encounter horses along this hike.

Drive US 101 north of the Golden Gate Bridge to Sir Francis Drake Highway and travel to the town of Olema. Take Highway 1 north and turn west onto Bear Valley Road. Drive 1.3 miles past the turnoff to Bear Valley Visitor Center, and then turn left onto Limantour Road. Go 5.7 miles and park just above the American Youth Hostel. The Coast Trail takes off from a gate just below the hostel. To reach the southernmost trailhead, drive south on Highway 1 for 8 miles, past

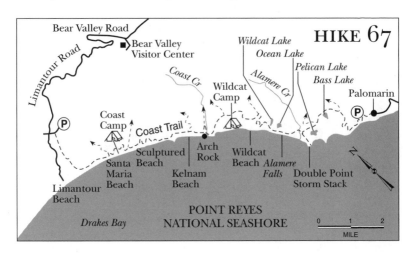

HIKE 67

Bear Valley Road

Bear Valley Visitor Center

Limantour Road

Coast Cr

Wildcat Lake

Ocean Lake

Alamere Cr

Pelican Lake

Bass Lake

Palomarin

Wildcat Camp

P

Coast Camp

Coast Trail

Santa Maria Beach

Sculptured Beach

Kelnam Beach

Arch Rock

Wildcat Beach

Alamere Falls

Double Point

Storm Stack

P

Limantour Beach

Drakes Bay

POINT REYES
NATIONAL SEASHORE

0   1   2
MILE

Olema. Take Olema/Bolinas Road (just north of Bolinas Lagoon), turn right on Mesa Road, and bear right where the pavement ends. Travel 1.3 miles to the signed Palomarin trailhead.

To start, follow the gentle, well-graded fire road (Coast Trail) alongside a mellow stream. Note the effects here of the huge Vision Fire of 1995—the neighboring coyote-brush-dotted hills are recovering rapidly from a major charring, while the alder- and willow-clogged riparian strip along this creek was left virtually intact. Cross the stream at 0.7 mile beneath a cluster of red alder trees. Random ferns, bush lupines, and coyote brush decorate the south banks, with horsetail and mint mingling with cattails. The stream gradually enlarges into a cattail-infested marsh. You soon reach smooth, sandy, and clean Limantour Beach at 1.8 miles. Shed your shoes for a promenade along a slender sand strip called Limantour Spit to the northwest. Appreciate the wonderful seaside close-ups on one side, and the estuary on the other. Then return to The Coast Trail by wandering into the grassy dunes that border the beach.

The steady rhythm of the ocean's waves and seagulls gliding over the perennial beach grasses that thrive on the bluffs accompany you over the next mile. Reach a thistle thicket and then a splendid eucalyptus specimen at a signed trailhead at 2.8 miles. Coast Camp, with fourteen sites, sits 150 yards to the south on a grassy bluff some 600 feet above Santa Maria Beach. The next 5 miles of Coast Trail roam a

Near Wildcat Beach, late winter

gentle and unassuming coastline, where soft fields coated with short grasses ascend modestly to rolling hillsides, and the views of Sculptured Beach, Kelnam Beach, and Arch Rock are frequent and inspiring. You're apt to see a few folks at large and chunky Arch Rock (8.6 miles), an extrusive rock outcrop. It's an ideal place for watching the scattered sea stacks attempting to block the waves that eventually cruise delicately over Kelnam Beach. Crawl through Arch Rock's tunnel if it's low tide.

The Coast Trail wanders along bluffs of coastal scrub to Wildcat Camp at 11.2 miles. Its twelve sites are near a small stream and are perched on a meadow overlooking strikingly spectacular and easily accessible Wildcat Beach. Spend some quality time finding and then watching Alamere Falls toppling over a cliff onto serene Wildcat Beach. It's best to watch this scene a couple of hundred yards away.

The trail then winds past orange bush monkeyflower and coyote brush and offers glimpses of twin shale outcroppings called Double Point. Don't miss the great views here of the sea stack Stormy Stack, before veering inland to reach Pelican Lake and then Bass Lake at 12.6 miles. The final 2.9 miles to the Palomarin trailhead consist of traipsing past canyons and terraces in a mixed forest of Douglas fir, bishop pine, and occasional blue oak.

68 ⚘ BRUSHY PEAKS AND BALD MOUNTAIN

Distance: 8.4-mile loop
Difficulty: Moderate to strenuous
High point: 2729 feet
Elevation gain: 1900 feet
Maps: USGS Kenwood, Rutherford
Nearest campground: Sugarloaf Ridge State Park, phone (707) 938-1519 or (707) 833-5712
Information: Sugarloaf Ridge State Park, phone (707) 938-1519 or (707) 833-5712

Few hikes offer solitude in addition to views of the coastline and expansive Napa Valley like this one. The route loops counterclockwise, mostly high atop ridges, but it also explores precious Sonoma Creek and meadows near the trip's start and finish. The Wappo Indian village of Wilikos once stood at Sonoma Creek's headwaters, which this

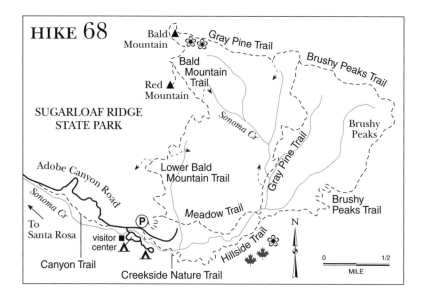

HIKE 68

SUGARLOAF RIDGE STATE PARK

Bald Mountain
Gray Pine Trail
Bald Mountain Trail
Red Mountain
Brushy Peaks Trail
Sonoma Cr
Brushy Peaks
Adobe Canyon Road
Lower Bald Mountain Trail
Sonoma Cr
To Santa Rosa
Gray Pine Trail
Brushy Peaks Trail
P
Meadow Trail
visitor center
Canyon Trail
Hillside Trail
Creekside Nature Trail
N
0   1/2
MILE

hike passes near and overlooks. The Wappo had several chiefs who were more like consultants, lending their expertise in specific areas such as ceremonials or medicine. The ridges you'll cover are steep, heavily clothed in a wide variety of native trees and shrubs, and contrast wonderfully with the flat and colorful Napa Valley.

Take this hike and then reward yourself by sampling wines at nearby Sonoma Valley's famous wineries. If it's late winter or early spring, be sure to take the 0.25 mile hike along Canyon Trail that reveals Sonoma Creek's gorgeous 25-foot long waterfall (pick up a park map from the visitor center). Lucky winter hikers might also encounter a new dusting of snow on the ridge tops. Mountain bikers and horses also use some of the trails along this hike.

From US 101 some 50 miles north of San Francisco in Santa Rosa, take Highway 12 east several miles to Adobe Canyon Road. Turn northeast and follow this paved and scenic road 3.4 twisting miles. Park just past the kiosk.

To start, take the Creekside Nature Trail next to the picnic tables. Numbered signposts correspond to the information in the park map available from the visitor center. This slender and shaded footpath follows part way up meandering Sonoma Creek before crossing a cement bridge in 0.5 mile. Fall is a serene time on this trail, which is lightly blanketed by a variety of crunching leaves. The creek in autumn is so quiet that it doesn't flow in some spots, revealing glimpses of human-sized boulders embedded in a neat gravel bottom.

Go left onto Hillside Trail, an old dirt road. It promptly begins a moderate climb, showing head-on views of Red Mountain and Mount Hood past tall specimens of Oregon white oaks. Black and coast live oaks soon become more common, accompanying you on a short descent to a long meadow that slopes gently down to Sonoma Creek. Irish green in the winter, this oak-dotted meadow becomes a vivid wildflower show in midspring.

Depart the meadow's edge and bear right onto signed Brushy Peaks Trail at 1.4 miles. Within a few yards, large and lush whiteleaf manzanita shrubs greet you in an open oak woodland scattered with fragrant evergreen California bay laurel. Occasional sparsely limbed Douglas firs and knee-high bracken ferns appear along the denser sections of the climb. Toward the ridge top, brushy clusters appear intermittently, featuring native shrubs such as chamise, orange bush monkeyflower, toyon, coyote brush, and manzanita. Occasional madrone trees crop up in the hardwood forest sections, which alternate with chaparral.

Reach a gap and a small clearing at 2.5 miles, featuring a southward view down into a broad and wooded canyon dotted with sloping vineyards. At 3.2 miles, the trail climbs up and down and up a trio of chaparral clad knobs called Brushy Peaks. Each one is a tad taller than the previous, and crossing them requires sharp descents followed by short, steep climbs. The first two crests yield intimate views of Red and Bald Mountains to the northwest and the numerous knolls and gaps comprising less wooded Sugarloaf Ridge to the west. Aptly named Bald Mountain is topped by short grasses that convert to golden in the fall. At 2243 feet, Brushy Peak proper features those views as part of a panorama that also reveals the rolling rows of hills to the east marching north to south. Note that the previously mentioned native trees and shrubs densely cloak Red Mountain and Mount Hood.

As the rest of the Brushy Peaks Trail stays mostly flat and winds northward along the ridge top, the totally flat and sprawling Napa Valley beckons to the east. Savor those views, for soon the slender footpath splits through an otherwise impenetrable thicket of brush. Reach a bountiful colony of gray pines that add a touch of gray to the already colorful mosaic along the ridge and upper slopes and then come to the signed Gray Pine Trail at 4.5 miles. Take this trail left to shorten this loop hike by almost 2 miles.

Chaparral view from Brushy Peaks, spring

Bear right along Gray Pine Trail and climb gently for 1.2 miles to reach Bald Mountain at almost 5.7 miles. Enjoy views that show off Mount St. Helena to the north, the ocean to the west (on clear days), and the previously mentioned gray forest from this photographic lookout. If you're in the mood for another peak, descend Bald Mountain Trail 0.4 mile to a right turn that leads 0.2 mile to Red Mountain. Bald Mountain Trail continues 1.4 miles and reaches Lower Bald Mountain Trail at about 7.2 miles. Turn left and return to your car.

NORTHERN
CALIFORNIA COAST

69 ⚘ RUSSIAN GULCH FALLS

Distance: 7.2-mile loop
Difficulty: Easy to moderate
High point: 450 feet
Elevation gain: 800 feet
Map: USGS Mendocino
Nearest campground: Russian Gulch State Park, phone (707) 937-5804
Information: Russian Gulch State Park, phone (707) 445-6547

The setting at Russian Gulch Falls is so divine that the thought of staying forever tends to cross the mind. Tucked way into a narrow canyon in a thick forest, these falls pound into a boulder basin, spraying cool mist in your face. An array of huge fallen logs furnish a lush green frame for the 35-foot-long waterfall, with some logs sprouting profuse ferns. The journey to this special spot delves deeper and deeper in a second growth redwood forest past little fern gullies to the falls, then traces the wild course of swift and clear Russian Gulch Creek. Solitude and whale watching are winter prizes on this hike, and the falls are in their prime by early spring. Cap the trip by crossing Highway 1 and walking the 1-mile loop to Devils Punch Bowl overlook.

From Highway 1 in Fort Bragg, head south for 6 miles to signed Russian Gulch State Park. Turn left and follow signs to the trailhead.

From the east end of the campground, get on signed North Trail, which climbs moderately for 0.5 mile through a dark and tranquil redwood forest interspersed with juvenile tan oak trees. Western sword ferns and California huckleberry comprise the understory, with an occasional patch of spring-blooming redwood sorrel.

At 0.7 mile, reach a small, rare stand of bishop pines and Mendocino cypresses on a crest at a trail junction. Continue straight here and again 0.2 mile father. Watch for a gigantic, triple-trunked and lightning-charred redwood near a wooden bench. North Trail descends a bit, then comes to a wooden bridge crossing a modest, meandering stream. A bit farther, check out a good-sized huckleberry shrub thriving inside a 6-by-6-foot redwood stump carved out by lightning.

The trail then promptly descends to some picnic benches alongside Russian Gulch Creek and the junction with signed Falls Loop Trail at 2.6 miles. It's best to go right onto the loop trail and walk it

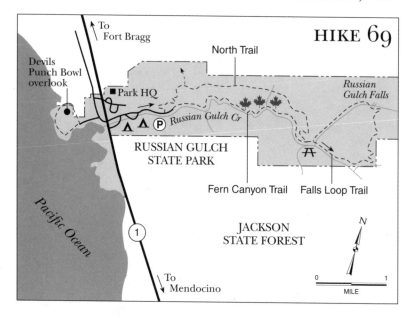

counterclockwise. This slightly longer route to the falls crosses rushing Russian Gulch Creek via a redwood-railed footbridge and climbs gently along one of the creek's forks for 0.7 mile. The trail then heads north in dense Douglas fir and hemlock forest for another 1.4 miles to reach Russian Gulch Falls at 4.7 miles. Although this side of the loop takes 1.4 miles longer to reach the falls, choosing it prolongs anticipation of the splendid cascade and also takes you down stone steps to reward you with an especially commanding view over the falls.

The trail drops to the foot of the pool where the falls are as wide as they are tall in the late winter and early spring. By autumn, when the bigleaf maples along Russian Gulch Creek turn gold, Russian Gulch Falls becomes a solo cascade with another stream formed on the left side of the rock.

The following 0.8 mile of dirt trail leaves the falls and continues counterclockwise, revealing hawk's-eye views down on the narrow and curving creek. When you reunite with the picnic area at 5.3 miles, continue on the paved and needle strewn Fern Canyon Trail. Heavily populated in the summer only, it hugs the maple- and alder-lined shores of Russian Gulch Creek for 1.9 miles.

When you reach the campground, take a brief break and then drive across Highway 1 to the headlands to explore 1 mile's worth of trails that show off Devils Punch Bowl. It's a 200-foot-long sea-cut tunnel that collapsed at its inland end to produce a 60-foot-deep hole that's about 100 feet across. Its steep walls are coated with lush green plants. Watch and wait for the occasional big waves (especially during winter storms) to pound the punch bowl's interior, creating eerie, throaty echoes. Choose from a series of trails that reach the edge of the bluff top to admire views of the dramatic rocky shoreline. If it's winter, gaze out on the ocean water for flopping and spouting California gray whales.

Russian Gulch Falls, early autumn

70 ✿ ARMSTRONG REDWOODS TO EAST AUSTIN CREEK

Distance: 14-mile figure-eight loop; 5.2-mile loop without the
Austin Creek area
Difficulty: Moderate
High point: 1200 feet
Elevation gain: 1900 feet
Map: USGS Guerneville
Nearest campground: Redwood Lake Campground, phone (707)
865-2391; occasionally closed for part of winter
Information: Austin Creek State Recreation Area, phone (707) 869-
2015 or (707) 865-2391

This hike could make you feel like an elf in a magical forest or an
imaginative Indian child in the Wild West. That's because it starts and
ends beneath spectacularly giant redwoods with the middle part roam-
ing over isolated, grassy hillsides dotted with oaks and keenly patrolled
by red-shouldered hawks.

Traipse in tranquil woods, looking down on a blanket of big redwood tops, and drink in wondrous views of lush and sprawling coastal
mountains. In the spring, deep forest wildflowers such as redwood sorrel, trillium, and redwood orchid are in full swing, and so are the open
grass slope wildflowers including lupine, wild iris, brodiaea, monkeyflower, filaree, clover, and buttercup. In autumn, when the black oaks
and bigleaf maples turn orange and yellow, most of the numerous
creeks on this trip are slow and quiet as the gray foxes and bobcats
that sneak in the bushes. But usually by midwinter, the creeks have
awakened and are as swift as the scurrying squirrel that hides acorns
and the western fence lizard that darts over rough boulders. Extend
your visit to this wonderland by staying overnight at one of the primitive backpacking camps. You may encounter mountain bikers and
horses along the trails.

Drive to Guerneville, 16 miles west of US 101 on River Road and
11 miles east of Highway 1 on Highway 116. Turn north at the stop
sign onto Armstrong Woods Road, drive 2.2 miles, and park in the
large paved lot.

Stop by the ranger station and pick up the leaflet for the self-
guided nature trail. Level Pioneer Trail features the 310-foot-tall Par-
son Jones redwood at the start, and soon reveals the 1,400-year-old
Colonel Armstrong redwood. Finish this short loop and then double

AUSTIN CREEK STATE
RECREATION AREA

HIKE 70

Austin Creek Trail

East Austin Cr

Mannings
Flat Camp

Thompson Cr

Tom King Camp

Bullfrog Pond Trail

Redwood
Lake CG

Redwood Lake

Gilliam Cr

Schoolhouse Cr

East Austin Cr

Gilliam
Creek Camp

Gilliam Cr Trail

East
Ridge
Trail

Pool
Ridge
Trail

Fife Cr

ARMSTRONG REDWOODS
STATE RESERVE

Pioneer
Trail

N

0   1
MILE

P

To
Guerneville ↘

back to get on Pool Ridge Trail. It follows Fife Creek awhile, first past
old growth redwoods and tan oak, and later past bigleaf maples and
California bay laurel. Farther yet, Douglas fir and madrone take over
as the redwoods diminish in size and number. The middle part of
Pool Ridge Trail switches between steep climbs and level stretches,
moving alternately through deep shade and sunny sites cloaked in
tall manzanita.

At about 2 miles into the trip, begin to climb moderately in deep
shade with occasional views to the east down into the heavily wooded
canyonsides. A half mile farther, go left on the Gilliam Creek Trail,
where the terrain changes noticeably. You promptly break into blue
oak, black oak, and coast live oak woodland and soon drop into
chaparral of manzanita, chamise, and toyon. This is a prime area for
finding the earth upturned by wild pig herds rummaging for bulbs,
buried nuts, and roots.

Buckeye tree in flower near Austin Creek Trail, midspring

Reach charming Schoolhouse Creek at 3.9 miles. Follow it for 0.4 mile, crossing this narrow stream three times before it finally reaches a wooden bridge and three-way junction. Head left here and follow Gilliam Creek's meandering course gently down to where it empties into larger East Austin Creek at 5.7 miles. If you're lucky enough to be backpacking, consider stopping here at Gilliam Creek Camp. Like the other two primitive campsites farther on, it has a table, wood stove, and pit toilet.

Follow a scenic stretch of East Austin Creek north then northwest, and be on the lookout for the colorful plumage of the wood duck, as well as great blue herons and white-tailed kites. Reach a junction with Austin Creek Trail and go left to reach Mannings Flat Camp, 2 miles beyond Gilliam Creek Camp. Stop here for a picnic, toe dipping in the creek, and bird-watching.

Retrace your steps on the Austin Creek Trail and cross Thompson Creek. A footpath heads left and climbs briefly and gently to Tom King Camp. The next couple of miles climb earnestly in mixed oak woodland, often with views down on East Austin Creek, and eventually westward across the open valley to the Coast Ranges.

At 12 miles, you reach the paved park road near Redwood Lake Campground. Follow a trail past Bullfrog Pond to a trail junction where you go left onto East Ridge Trail. This trail mirrors Pool Ridge Trail across the road, but it goes downhill for the 2.5 miles to the trailhead.

71 ⚘ LOST COAST: BEAR HARBOR TO USAL CAMPGROUND

Distance: 33 miles round trip; 16.5 miles one-way
Difficulty: Strenuous
High point: 1000 feet
Elevation gain: 10,600 feet
Map: Sinkyone Wilderness State Park map
Nearest campground: Nadelos Campground, phone (707) 825-2300
Information: Sinkyone Wilderness State Park, phone (707) 445-6547 or (707) 986-7711

Most folks only dream of getting around to taking this classic trip in Sinkyone Wilderness State Park, but once you've experienced the Lost Coast, the memory will forever be etched in your soul. It's a rare coastal wilderness experience featuring stout redwoods, jaw-dropping perpendicular views of black sand beaches (almost 1000 feet down in places), and flashes of wildflowers coating grassy summits.

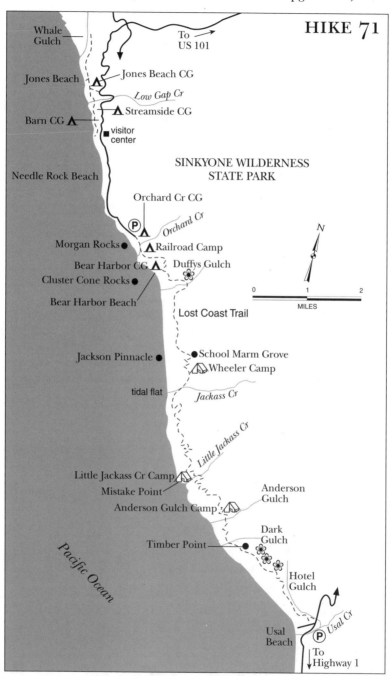

HIKE 71

Whale Gulch

To US 101

Jones Beach CG

Jones Beach

Low Gap Cr

Streamside CG

Barn CG

visitor center

Needle Rock Beach

SINKYONE WILDERNESS STATE PARK

Orchard Cr CG

Orchard Cr

Morgan Rocks

Railroad Camp

Bear Harbor CG

Duffys Gulch

Cluster Cone Rocks

Bear Harbor Beach

Lost Coast Trail

N

0   1   2
MILES

Jackson Pinnacle

School Marm Grove

Wheeler Camp

tidal flat

Jackass Cr

Little Jackass Cr

Little Jackass Cr Camp

Anderson Gulch

Mistake Point

Anderson Gulch Camp

Dark Gulch

Timber Point

Hotel Gulch

Usal Cr

Usal Beach

To Highway 1

Pacific Ocean

This is the land just south of Kings Peak, which at 4086 feet above sea level is the tallest peak on the Northern California coast. Brown pelicans swoop over the shiny sea at sunset, and Cape Mendocino, the state's westernmost point, juts to the north. The active San Andreas Fault lies just offshore, making for an untamed and sensational scenario of precipitous, irregular, and unpredictable cliffs. Many of the shrubs and wildflowers are in peak bloom in spring. You'll most likely encounter solitude in the winter and clearest views in the fall. Alas, paradise sometimes comes with a hefty price. Pack lightly, for you'll surely be sweating like a boxer in the tenth round and wheezing like a donkey while climbing the numerous fern-covered canyonsides. If time is short and energy is low, arrange for a car to meet you at Usal Campground, thus chopping the trip in half.

This hike is so isolated you might feel you're the only soul left in the world. However, not long ago, this rugged and wild area was heavily impacted by humans. Many of the marine terraces and upper grasslands once pastured sheep and cattle. Lost Coast's trail systems are actually old railroad lines, pack mule pathways (for hauling tan oak), and logging roads. For several centuries before European settlement, the Sinkyone Indians expertly hunted Roosevelt elk (some herds still exist here), grizzly bear, and sea lions. They also used redwood for building canoes and lean-tos. All the numerous Sinkyone Indian villages that once bordered this hike's many creeks featured ceremonial dances and sweat lodges.

Lost Coast Trail, winter

Drive US 101 to Redway, about 60 miles south of Eureka. Travel 12 miles on Briceland Road and turn left at Whitethorn. After 4 miles, go straight at the Four Corners junction onto a dirt road labeled County Road 435, and drive 3.6 miles to the visitor center. The next 2.4 miles to the Bear Harbor trailhead are very narrow, potholed, and winding. To reach Usal Campground, drive to Leggett on US 101 and then take Highway 1 west for several miles. Look for County Road 431 (also known as Usal Road) on the right at mile marker 90.88. Turn right and drive this road north for 6 miles.

Begin at the northernmost trailhead near Orchard Creek Campground. This campground is very small and often full. Cross slim Orchard Creek beneath a cluster of tall red alders, pass Railroad Camp at 0.2 mile, and continue on Lost Coast Trail along the creek and into a meadow decorated by horsetails. Spend some time at Bear Harbor, where there's an excellent campsite and a knoll revealing breathtaking views up and down the Lost Coastline. Watch the big waves crash against Cluster Cone Rocks, some sea stacks resembling Tibetan mountaintops.

The trail wanders east next to a gulch laden with sword fern and cow parsnip beneath towering red alder. California bay laurel shows up near a stream crossing, shading redwood sorrel and profuse sword fern. Higher up, the clean evergreen foliage of California huckleberry shrubs takes center stage. Cross shaded Duffys Gulch at 2.2 miles, where a peaceful brook babbles gracefully over mossy boulders beneath a massive bigleaf maple and some old growth redwoods.

The trail then leads past grassland awash in spring with lupines, blue-eyed grass, and poppies, to steep bluffs overlooking the sea. Pass a garden of orange bush monkeyflower before alternating between grasslands and dark forests until reaching an almost pure redwood forest at 3.3 miles. More old growth redwoods highlight cool and tranquil School Marm Grove, named after the former Wheeler Schoolhouse nearby. Pass Wheeler Camp and reach Jackass Creek at 4.8 miles. Just beyond the creek sits the abandoned logging town of Wheeler, now a collection of old bridge remnants and crumbling cement foundations.

Some heavy-duty up and down climbing ensues over the next 8 miles to exquisite vistas at Timber Point. At 9 miles, Sally Bell Grove features campsites at Little Jackass Creek. Majestic old growth redwoods shade two sites and a couple of more sites border a shiny black sand beach. Capture the photogenic views of Anderson Cliffs to the south from Mistake Point, where you can look down on barking sea lions swimming near a pretty, pocket beach.

Reach Timber Point at 12.6 miles, and the rest of the journey is a cakewalk compared to the fern-coated canyons you've just climbed in and out of. Lost Coast Trail stays mostly flat along the grassy ridges (more lupines in the spring), showing occasional glimpses of a staggered file of beautiful bluffs and steep cliffs. The final 2 miles plunge rapidly to Usal Campground, featuring a big beach, a meadow, and smooth-flowing Usal Creek.

72 ⚮ EEL RIVER WILDLIFE AREA AND BEACH

Distance: 9.4 miles round trip
Difficulty: Easy to moderate
High point: 30 feet
Elevation gain: 300 feet
Map: USGS Tyee City
Nearest campground: Patricks Point State Park, phone (707) 677-3570
Information: Humboldt County Parks Department, phone (707) 445-7652

Get lost in a daydream while strolling isolated Table Bluff Beach, admire harbor seals living at the mouth of the Eel River, and then return along a secluded sand spit featuring well-preserved sand dunes, a protected wildlife area, and a long and slender bay.

The Wiyot Indians once had a settlement on Table Bluff. Settlers in the 1850s established a modest agricultural community, and large, old, run-down barns remain on the sloping fields at the hike's start. A lighthouse built on Table Bluff in the late 1800s has been removed,

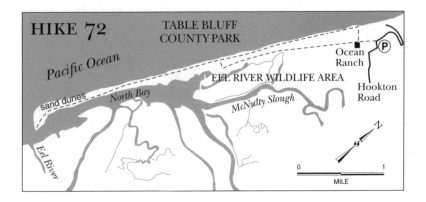

but the large bluff-top edge is still a great lookout. Enjoy more birds and solitude in the winter, but come in the fall for the clearest views. Horses are allowed along this hike.

From US 101 a few miles south of Eureka, turn west on paved Hookton Road. Drive 5 miles and park on the side of the road near two old gates at the big bend.

Enter Table Bluff County Park and follow an old dirt jeep track south toward a good-looking barn for 200 yards. Then veer toward the ocean on another old jeep road to access the beach.

The dark and sandy beach stretches south as far as the eye can see. Stroll aimlessly and barefoot along this slender and secluded loop hike. The idea is to stay intimate with the surf and to keep the sometimes cold and annoying north breezes at your back. Avoid these strong winds on your return trip by walking through the bumpy and sagging sand dunes a long touchdown pass from the beach.

Low tide is a special bonus. Roam the foam and look eastward at two tiers: The flat beach landscape scattered with big driftwood stumps and limbs occupies the front row and shiny grass-covered sand dunes are higher up. Gain better footing by traipsing on the wet sand closest to the tide. Even this very fine sand tends to sink deeper than sands on other beaches. Rest assured your arches and heels will get massaged, stretched, and worked out.

The setting is so open and spacious in all directions, and the rhythm of the waves is so contagious, you're apt to wander dazed, but not confused, for up to an hour before pausing to sniff the salty sea air and admire the panorama. Far inland, the smooth foothills and more angular coastal mountains are often topped with puffy cumulus clouds on clear days, common in autumn.

At 4.7 miles, you reach the mouth of the Eel River. To make this a shorter trip, cross the dunes at any point and wander back to the trailhead. You'll still be able to explore part of North Bay if you turn around at 2.3 miles.

Your return route from the mouth of Eel River is pleasingly different, featuring spectacular postcardlike countryside scenery. Stay close to and follow slender North Bay at first. Check out the flight patterns of the wide variety of shore, water, and land birds that help make Eel River Wildlife Area special. You may spot a black-tailed jackrabbit hopping near the shoreline. The calm bay curves, swirls, widens, and shrinks, and gorgeous driftwood specimens deposited long ago beyond the beach and dunes make for great photos in front of North Bay.

Table Bluff Beach, spring

Reach a wide marshy area, leave the bay shoreline, and promptly pick up a sandy jeep road that escorts you through the middle of expansive sand dunes awash with striking coastal native wildflowers. These include beach strawberry, yellow sand verbena, sea rocket, bush lupine, beach morning glory, and northern dune tansy.

73 ARCATA MARSH AND WILDLIFE SANCTUARY

Distance: 2.7-mile loop
Difficulty: Easy
High point: 20 feet
Elevation gain: 100 feet
Map: USGS Arcata South
Nearest campground: Patricks Point State Park, phone (707) 445-6547 or (707) 677-3570
Information: Environmental Services Department, City of Arcata, phone (707) 822-5953

To create a natural bird-watcher's paradise, combine a large saltwater bay, a nearby ocean, freshwater and saltwater marshes, a lake, a pond,

mudflats, streams, and foothills. This is the unique setting of Arcata Marsh and Wildlife Sanctuary, which provides all these habitats to make a haven for some 200 bird species. No wonder it's the most popular bird-watching area in Northern California. You're apt to meet some serious ornithologists here, complete with binoculars, notepads, tripods, and zoom lenses. In fact, the local Audubon Society leads guided tours of the sanctuary on Saturday mornings at 8:30, starting from the parking lot. Plan on spending 3 to 4 hours here, and treat this sanctuary as a stage, starring hundreds of birds dipping, diving, soaring, gliding, and paddling. All you have to do is wander the several looping, wide, flat, and wheelchair-accessible gravel or bark paths.

From US 101 in Arcata, take the Samoa Boulevard exit (Highway 255). Go west for 0.3 mile and turn south (left) on South I Street. Follow it less than 1 mile to its end at a large, paved parking lot with picnic tables and restrooms.

To start, follow part of Humboldt Bay, which is an expansive coastal mudflat. It's extremely rich in nutrients and looks like soup covered with film. This northernmost section of the bay is a cross between slimy mud and shallow gray pools that fluctuate with the tide. At low tide, it's meal time for godwits, egrets, herons, sanderlings, sandpipers, and curlews. At nearby Klopp Lake (stocked with rainbow trout), look for cormorants, coots, ducks, and seven species of gulls.

Cattails and willows at Arcata Marsh, spring

Soon you reach the cluster of marshes, which support black phoebes, kingfishers, sparrows, ospreys, and marsh wrens. Although these marshlands seem extensive today, 6,000 acres of them were filled for industrial, residential, and agricultural development. Long ago, the coastal Indians depended heavily on the abundant, life-sustaining food from these marshes, using natural materials for boats, tools, and dwellings. Several large interpretive signs detail the local and natural history of these marshes, with some showing pictures of the more common land and shore birds.

Some of the marshlands are blanketed with alders, willows, and blackberry bushes. If visiting in early fall, look for ripe berries. Other sections are coated with abundant native aquatic plants and pea green scum. Clusters of cattails sway in the breeze on small islands.

74 ⚑ BIG LAGOON AND AGATE BEACH

Distance: 9 miles
Difficulty: Easy to moderate
High point: 250 feet
Elevation gain: 400 feet
Map: USGS Trinidad
Nearest campground: Patricks Point State Park, phone (707) 445-6547 or (707) 677-3570
Information: Patricks Point State Park, phone (707) 445-6547 or (707) 677-3570

From just south of Trinidad and on up to Crescent City, there are several great beaches, and Agate Beach is definitely one of them. Stretching northeast for several miles, this pristine beach doesn't feature the ocean sea stacks that are just around the corner to the west at Patricks Point. It does boast some surprisingly big waves—in fact swimming is dangerous due to the robust surf, sleeper waves, and rip currents. Wander the length of the beach for a total trip of 9 miles, or turn around at any point to shorten the trip. You decide.

Popular in the summer, Agate Beach is in its prime when you're the only one there, trudging wet and free during a cleansing winter rain. After storms is the best time to collect black jade and agate polished by the waves and cast upon the beach. Springtime is special for the steep hillside coated with flowering lupine. Autumn is the most photogenic, when it's more likely to be clear.

Drive US 101 about 30 miles north of Eureka to the exit for Patricks Point State Park (also signed for Patricks Point Drive). Take this exit and follow signs into the park. Then follow signs for Agate Beach, with its large, paved parking lot.

At the start of the hike, a wide dirt path drops 300 feet over 0.25 mile to the southwestern edge of Agate Beach. The views of the evenly tilted, yellow gray sandstone cliffs rising suddenly above the beach are tremendous. The lakelike setting of Big Lagoon caps the scene in the distance and is separated from the sea by a long and shiny sand spit. This descent to the beach proceeds past dense salal shrubs shaded by tall Sitka spruce trees.

When you reach the beach, notice the timid creek that trickles over basketball-sized boulders and then abruptly disappears into the sand and gravel. Take the short spur trail that ventures up this stream past a couple of small and clear pools. For the first 0.6 mile, the nearly vertical and mostly barren cliffs of sandstone strata take center stage, topped by wind-sculpted conifers.

The westernmost section of Agate Beach is modestly littered with driftwood twigs and is composed of wave-polished gravel in three basic sizes—pea, marble, and half-dollar-sized skipping discs. Sand gets mixed in more after about 0.6 mile, but it's further from the tide, bordering the cliffs, where sand castles are apt to last longer before getting washed away. People tend to get scarce about 0.3 mile farther, as the cliff faces taper noticeably to a union with Big Lagoon, still 1 mile away.

Seagulls circle endlessly, gently scouting the boundless sea. The cliffs are at their steepest starting at 1.3 miles along the beach, where

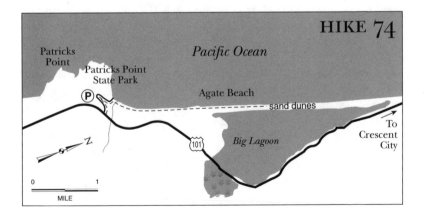

HIKE 74

Patricks Point

Pacific Ocean

Patricks Point State Park

Agate Beach

sand dunes

To Crescent City

Big Lagoon

0   1

MILE

Ceremonial Rock in Patricks Point State Park, spring

a handful of posh abodes near the edge are threatened by erosion. The cliffs are more noticeably rust- and orange-colored where water pours from a corroded pipe at 1.8 miles.

At 2.1 miles, Big Lagoon contrasts greatly with what's now behind you. Bluffs and grayish brown sand is the scene here. Dark blue Big Lagoon, where sailing regattas are held, is bordered on the other side by conifer-clothed coastal hills, adding variety to the hike's views. It's best to stroll the highest level of the sand spit for awhile to gain views of the ocean and the lagoon with a simple head turn. Consider darting over to the lagoon's edge to explore its curving beach as you head north for up to 2.4 miles. Then return along the ocean for constant views of Patricks Point.

75 SMITH RIVER AND LITTLE BALD HILLS

Distance: 13 miles round trip; 5.5 miles round trip to Stout Grove
Difficulty: Moderate to strenuous
High point: 1900 feet
Elevation gain: 2000 feet
Map: USGS Hiouchi
Nearest campground: Jedediah Smith Campground, phone (707) 458-3310
Information: Jedediah Smith Redwoods State Park, phone (707) 464-9533 or (707) 458-3310

It's not hard to feel small as an ant wandering beneath this journey's towering redwoods. You might also feel wild as a bobcat prowling the

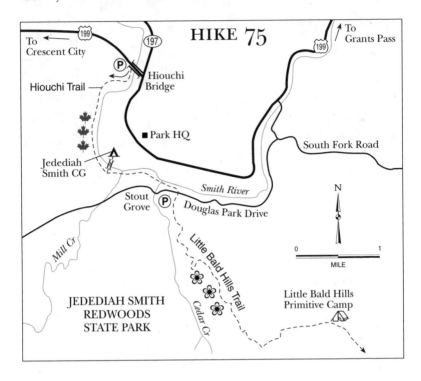

banks of the Smith River, California's largest undammed river. It's also a good river for fishing. This ambitious hike follows pure and wild Smith River all the way to a beach, then ducks deep into an even larger redwood forest (Stout Grove). This is what mighty and ancient redwoods looked like in the dinosaur age. From there, an old mining route climbs to a ridge laden with serpentine soils, which support a wide array of native plants. You can also see the ocean in the distance from the top.

Following fall's first cold spell, the leaves of the occasional vine maples turn crimson along sections of this hike. In winter and early spring, parts of Smith River become major torrents, creating a noisy and active scene. The same is true of Mill Creek, which most of the time can be crossed barefoot and with rolled up pants (call ahead for up-to-date trail conditions). By midspring, there's a colorful mosaic of native wildflowers adorning the stone-stippled grassland that tops Little Bald Hills. Look for California Indian pink, phlox, and blue-headed gilia.

Drive just north of Crescent City on US 101 and go east on Highway 199. After 4.1 miles, park on the west side of the Hiouchi Bridge.

Begin along shaded and mostly flat Hiouchi Trail, which soon leads to a pristine view of river ripples and a large gravel beach (a spur trail leads down to the river). Enter a mixed forest of California bay laurel, madrone, redwood, tan oak, and rhododendron, and reach a railed overlook at 0.8 mile. Look down on one of steady flowing Smith River's many gravel islands. These are ideal spots for spawning salmon to lay eggs.

Secluded and well-designed Hiouchi Trail makes a handful of slight rises and falls over the next mile, but always stays within eye- and earshot of gently curving Smith River. Pass another overlook at 1.9 miles, followed by a benchland featuring vine maple and alder. Pass a bridge on the left that leads to Jedediah Smith Campground, and then cross Mill Creek at its photogenic meeting with Smith River.

Enter an alluvial flat that furnishes shelter and rich soil for Stout Grove's old growth redwood belt. Cross a rustic wooden bridge, highlighted by vine maple, where Cedar Creek empties into Smith River. Cross Douglas Park Drive at 3.2 miles, where the trail becomes Little Bald Hills Trail. Note some large redwoods that have amazingly survived despite being damaged by lightning. Listen for the squeaky-brake chirp of the varied thrush in this redwood forest, with huckleberry, rhododendron, and salal shrub accompaniment.

Smith River, early autumn

The trail flattens along a modest streambed clogged with alders and then climbs steadily in a hardwood forest of tan oak and bay laurel. Douglas fir enters the mix, followed by gray-needled Port Orford cedar, which is rare in Northern California.

Reach a series of clearings at 4.6 miles, where Jeffrey pines decorate an open woodland. Chaparral such as manzanita, coffeeberry, and young madrones add food sources for the dry-dwelling wildlife. Hunting by animals is prevalent here. Bears snare fish from Smith River, the spotted owl patrols the redwood forest at night, while coyote, mountain lion, and bobcat sneak around the chaparral.

At 6.2 miles, a spur trail goes left to Little Bald Hills Primitive Camp, which should be as far as your pack goes, even though you may day hike a few miles farther. Fleeting glances of the ocean soon appear past conifer-clad canyons and mountainsides. The Little Bald Hills proper (about 7 miles into the trip) are grasslands that underwent planned periodic fires by Native Americans. These indigenous people knew that fires would increase useful plants and increase beneficial fungi and bacteria in the soil.

TRAIL INDEX

| Autumn 🍁 | Winter ❄ | Spring ❀ |
| Hikes with Children 🚶🚶 | Backpack Trips 🥾🥾 | Bird-Watching 🦆 |

Hike Name

Big Bear Lake, spring

INDEX

ABOUT THE AUTHOR

Marc Soares is a landscape consultant and teaches plant and yoga classes for Shasta College Community Education. He is a professional outdoor photographer and naturalist who writes columns for the *Redding Record Searchlight* newspaper. He also plays guitar and sings in a local classic rock band. Marc also has written two other hiking guidebooks, *100 Classic Hikes in Northern California* (The Mountaineers Books, 2000) and *Best Coast Hikes of Northern California: A Guide to the Top Trails from Big Sur to the Oregon Border* (Sierra Club, 1998).

THE MOUNTAINEERS, founded in 1906, is a nonprofit outdoor activity and conservation club, whose mission is "to explore, study, preserve, and enjoy the natural beauty of the outdoors . . . . " Based in Seattle, Washington, the club is now the third-largest such organization in the United States, with 15,000 members and five branches throughout Washington state.

The Mountaineers sponsors both classes and year-round outdoor activities in the Pacific Northwest, which include hiking, mountain climbing, ski-touring, snowshoeing, bicycling, camping, kayaking and canoeing, nature study, sailing, and adventure travel. The club's conservation division supports environmental causes through educational activities, sponsoring legislation, and presenting informational programs. All club activities are led by skilled, experienced volunteers, who are dedicated to promoting safe and responsible enjoyment and preservation of the outdoors.

If you would like to participate in these organized outdoor activities or the club's programs, consider a membership in The Mountaineers. For information and an application, write or call The Mountaineers, Club Headquarters, 300 Third Avenue West, Seattle, WA 98119; 206-284-6310.

The Mountaineers Books, an active, nonprofit publishing program of the club, produces guidebooks, instructional texts, historical works, natural history guides, and works on environmental conservation. All books produced by The Mountaineers are aimed at fulfilling the club's mission.

Send or call for our catalog of more than 450 outdoor titles:

The Mountaineers Books
1001 SW Klickitat Way, Suite 201
Seattle, WA 98134
800-553-4453
mbooks@mountaineers.org
www.mountaineersbooks.org

Other titles you may enjoy from The Mountaineers Books:

THE HIGH SIERRA: Peaks, Passes, and Trails, 2nd Edition, *R.J. Secor*
An updated version of the only book to cover all known mountain and trail routes on more than 570 Sierra Peaks; details permit information, safety, and history.

CLIMBING CALIFORNIA'S FOURTEENERS: 183 Routes to the Fifteen Highest Peaks, *Stephen F. Porcella & Cameron M. Burns*
The only guide that offers multiple routes, from walk-ups to screamers, on all fifteen mountains, complete with historical notes and commentary from John Muir, Norman Clyde, and Clarence King.

CALIFORNIA STATE PARKS: A Complete Recreation Guide,
George & Rhonda Ostertag
Features complete details on more than 200 parks and state-managed outdoor areas, encompassing everything from the ocean to the mountains to the desert.

BEST SHORT HIKES IN AND AROUND THE NORTH SACRAMENTO VALLEY, *John R. Soares*
75 short walks and day-hiking getaways all within an hour's drive of the Valley.

50 CLASSIC BACKCOUNTRY SKI AND SNOWBOARD SUMMITS IN CALIFORNIA, *Paul Richins, Jr.*
The most comprehensive guide available, complete with a superb mix of routes for both intermediate and expert backcountry skiers and snowboarders. Routes range in location from Mount Shasta to Mount Whitney.

ADVENTURE CYCLING IN™ NORTHERN CALIFORNIA,
The Adventure Cycling Association
44 classic rides that range from one-day to multi-day tours are presented with information on level of difficulty, terrain, traffic, best time to ride, points of interest, accommodations, and more.

BEST SHORT HIKES IN CALIFORNIA'S NORTHERN SIERRA: A Guide to Day Hikes near Campgrounds, *Karen & Terry Whitehill*
74 trails situated between the San Joaquin/Mammoth area and Donner Pass that guarantee hiking satisfaction with features such as outstanding views, swimming holes, and stunning wildlife.